# THE MAGIC OF SAND DOLLARS

A NOVEL BY
## JUDITH A. PERKINS

EXPLORA BOOKS
700 – 838 West Hastings St. Vancouver, BC V6C 0A6
www.explorabooks.com
Phone: (604) 330 6795

ISBN: 978-1-997587-27-9 (Paperback)
978-1-997587-28-6 (eBook)

# THE
# MAGIC OF
# SAND DOLLARS

## JUDITH A. PERKINS

# *Contents*

# Chapter 1

"Maybe I will change, Mama. I am not really comfortable in this suit. I have another one that is more comfortable."

It was June 1983, and Maggie was eager to get her bathing suit on and head for the beach. A whole bunch of her friends from school were meeting there for a party to celebrate the end of the school year.

"Maggie, you will have to take Nicky with you today. I am depending on you to watch him this summer," Vickie announced.

"Mom," Maggie cried. "I am meeting my friends there. I will be mortified if I have to bring him along. Everyone will laugh at me."

"There is nothing else to do, Maggie! I have to go to work, and Nicky cannot stay at home by himself. Your dad won't be home until after 6 tonight."

"Oh, Mom! Why can't I ever have a life of my own? Why do I always have to look after him?" Maggie cried. "He is really a pain and doesn't listen to me anyway."

"Maggie, you know that my job is on the line right now. I am having to learn a new cash register system as well as manage the other cashiers. If I can't do the job efficiently, they will fire me," Vickie was trying to explain to her daughter.

"Why do you have to work anyway? My friends' mothers stay at home during the day. My friends don't have to babysit their little brothers. Only I do!" Maggie said in an angry voice.

As Vickie was trying to get ready to go to work, she said in an angry voice, "Maggie, do you want decent clothes? Do you want to be able to go to a movie with your friends occasionally? Do you want to be able to eat a decent meal? Well, my salary helps you do that, so quit complaining about your life and look after Nicky today. No more talk about it."

Maggie gave her mother a nasty look and stomped out of her bedroom. "And make your bed!" her mother shouted after her.

Maggie stomped into her bedroom, pulled the sheets and blanket up on her bed, and changed into her other bathing suit. It looked a little sexier, and there was a boy in her class she really wanted to impress. She didn't know how she was going to do it with Nicky around, but she would try. Maybe the little twerp would find a friend he could play with.

Dan had gone to work early that morning. He had one of his logging trucks down, and he had to get it fixed. He had a big order to bring into the mill and couldn't afford to be late with it. The Florence Lumber Mill needed the logs right away. Dan was always very prompt with his orders, and the mill depended on him to bring the orders in on time. Because one of his trucks was down, he was worried that he could deliver all of the needed logs today. "I am hoping that it is just a minor problem and I can get it fixed this morning and still get the order to the mill on time," he told his wife as he was leaving the house for the office. Vickie gave him a kiss on the cheek and a hug for encouragement. She knew he was a good mechanic and took excellent care of his equipment. She had great confidence in her husband and his abilities to provide for the family. Right now, because of the economy in the Florence area, she had to work to supplement their income. The kids were growing so fast and always seemed to need new shoes or new coats, and unfortunately, they both needed them at the same time.

IGA had just recently purchased and installed a new cash register system that was run by a computer. Vickie did not know very much about computers and didn't understand how they worked, so she was having a hard time understanding the new system and how it was going to work. She was the head cashier and had to make sure that the others knew how to run the registers efficiently. If she couldn't, then she would not be able to supervise the rest of the cashiers. She was really stressing out about her job, and on top of that, Maggie was making waves about having to watch Nicky. Usually, Nicky went over to Beth's house next door. Beth had a son just a year younger than Nick, and they were good friends. Vickie would let Beth know when she got home, and Nick would come home then, but Beth was sick with a bad cold and fever, and Josh, her son, had gone into Eugene to stay with his grandma until his mother got better and could take care of him. So, Nick was at loose ends, and Maggie had to watch out for him.

Today was the worst day to have him tagging along. She really wanted to impress Josh and make him notice her. Some of the other girls in her class had boyfriends, and she wanted one too. It was really neat to have a boy walk down the halls of the school with you. She had even seen a boy and girl kissing in front of a classroom before he left to go to his class. Maggie thought that would have been the neatest thing to do.

"Come on, pest. I want to get to the beach before a lot of the others do. I want to get a good spot to put my towel and bag. Take your stuff, Nick!" Maggie told him. "You will need a towel and your shirt. You cannot get a bad sunburn again. You know how it hurts. I have some of this goop that Mom puts on you. I will rub it on you when we get down there."

"I don't know why I have to have a babysitter anyway. I am old enough to look after myself," Nick mumbled as he followed behind his sister. He wanted to be at the beach, but he certainly didn't want to have to follow his sister around all day. Most of his friends had gone for short trips to celebrate the end of the school year, and no one was around this weekend.

Sometimes when Nick wasn't in school, Dan would take him to the office with him. Nick knew the rules when he went with his dad, and he knew his boundaries at the lumber yard. He was very good at staying out of the way. Most of the time, he stayed in the office or on the porch watching the workings of the yard. He loved to watch the logs being loaded onto the trucks. He wanted to learn to operate one of the large cranes that loaded the logs one day.

Maggie found the perfect spot to put her towel down on the sand. There was a fairly large log behind her, and she would be able to lean up against it and show off her new bathing suit. Nick was starting to put his towel down beside hers, but she stopped him.

"No, you spread your towel over there," she said, indicating a spot several feet away from the group gathering around the log.

Nick stomped over to the place Maggie indicated, laid his towel down, and plopped down on it with a dejected look on his face. What was he going to do now? There didn't seem to be anyone around for him to play with.

Maggie soon became involved in conversations with her friends, and the new boy, Josh, came up and spread his towel down next to her, and Vickie soon forgot about having to watch Nick. She was engrossed in talking to her friend and impressing Josh. Someone had brought a battery-operated tape player, and they had music to listen to.

As usual, it was loud, and even if Nick had needed her, she wouldn't have heard him.

Nick was bored after five minutes of sitting on his towel. He put his shirt on because he didn't want to get a sunburn. He had had one before, and it was very bad, and the doctor said that his skin was very sensitive to the sun and he should always have sunscreen cream rubbed on him and wear a shirt. Maggie forgot to put the cream on him, and he didn't want to go over there now. He would be embarrassed if he had to ask her to rub cream on him in front of all those big kids.

He decided to take a walk down the beach and see if he could find any neat shells or unbroken sand dollars. They were neat, and he was getting a pretty good collection of them. He found a stick that he could dig with, left his towel, but took his bag with him to put his treasures in and started walking down the beach. He walked down towards the waterline. Sometimes he would find good sand dollars that had just washed up from the ocean. When he and his mom would go into some of the gift stores along the highway, he noticed that people would paint scenes on the sand dollars. He figured that he could sell some of his to those stores and make some money. He really wanted an airplane that he could fly with a remote control, but they were very expensive, and his dad said that they couldn't afford one of them now. Maybe he could earn the money himself.

Maggie was busy with her friends and didn't notice that Nick was gone. About an hour after they had arrived at the beach, she dug into her bag for a candy bar and felt the bottle of sun lotion she was supposed to rub on Nick. She pulled it up out of her bag, looked over to where Nick's towel was laying on the sand, and didn't see him anywhere around it. She looked up and down the beach, but he was nowhere in sight. He had a pair of red bathing trunks on, so she thought that she would see him easily.

"Hey, everyone, has anyone seen my little brother?" Maggie hollered to the crowd. "He was sitting on that towel over there a few minutes ago."

They all either shook their heads or hollered 'no' to Maggie. "Darn kid," she thought to herself and muttered under her breath that now she would have to leave her friends to go look for him. He was bound to ruin her whole day at the beach. This was supposed to be a day of celebration at the end of the school year. No more being low man on the totem pole at school. She would be a sophomore next year.

As Maggie walked down the beach, she looked everywhere for Nick and didn't see him anywhere. She saw a kid in red trunks, but it wasn't her brother. She was really getting frustrated and very angry at him for leaving when she saw a commotion farther down the beach, near the waterline. She started walking towards the crowd of people, sure that she would find Nick there. He was always sticking his nose into other people's business and would probably be doing just that now.

"What's going on?" Maggie asked a man who was standing there in the crowd. She couldn't see over all the people. "Apparently, some kid got pulled into the water by an undertow. Fortunately, he was pushed back to the shore by the tide."

Maggie turned white as a sheet. She pushed her way through the crowd. "Let me through. I have to see who that is," she screamed at people. She caught a glimpse of a pair of red bathing trunks and almost fainted. "I think that is my brother. Let me through, please," she begged.

Some people were working on him, trying to get him to breathe.

"Nick!" Maggie cried. "Nick, wake up. It's time to wake up. I have to put this cream on you. Nick, wake up," she kept crying to him. Finally, Nick took a gasp of air and expelled a whole bunch of water. The people working on him laid him over on his side, and he kept throwing up seawater, but he was breathing in between throwing up. "Nick! Please talk to me. It's Maggie. I was looking for you. Why didn't you tell me you were leaving?"

Nick looked at his sister and started crying. "Maggie, you are hurting my hand," he said as he tried to pull his fingers out of her hand. Maggie let loose, but still held his hand gently.

"We are going to take him to the doctor and make sure he is okay. He swallowed a lot of seawater. It might be a good idea if you called his mom and dad. The doctor will want to talk to them," one of the men told her.

"Okay. I will call my mom. She works at the IGA in town," Maggie answered.

There was not a phone nearby that she could use to call either her mom or dad, so she ran all the way up the beach and up to the IGA store. It was closer than her home. As she ran into the store, Vickie saw her and the panicked look on her face.

"What's wrong? Where's Nicky?" Vickie cried.

"He was hurt, Mom. They have taken him to the doctor. They need you there."

Vickie looked at the girl at the next register. "You go! I will take care of things here." When Vickie hesitated, looking towards the boss's office, the other cashier said, "Go! I will take care of him."

Vickie grabbed her purse and ran out of the store, followed by Maggie. They jumped into Vickie's car and headed towards the doctor's office.

Vickie was trying to find out what had happened, but Maggie was crying so much she couldn't get anything out. All she said was that he walked away and didn't tell her where he was going. She didn't mention that she had forgotten him and left him to fend for himself on the beach for over an hour before she realized that he was gone.

The doctor came out of the exam room just as Vickie was going in. She asked, "Where is Nick?" she demanded. "Vickie, he is okay," Doc Jansen said as he held her by the shoulders. "I want you to calm down a bit before you go in and see him. Right now, he is drowsy. I gave him a very light sedative so he would rest. He was pretty agitated when he came in."

"What happened? Maggie was so upset, she couldn't tell me anything," Vickie said.

"You were lucky, Vickie. A couple of paramedics from Eugene just happened to be on the beach when Nick was pulled out by an undertow. Somehow, the tide pushed him back onto the beach. They saw it happen and rushed down to the water to grab him before he was pulled out again. They pulled him up and started administering aid right away and got him in here soon after he started vomiting seawater," Doc explained.

Vickie turned around to look at her daughter and asked, "Where were you? Why wasn't he with you?"

"Mom, he walked away from the group. I looked for him, but I couldn't find him. I walked all the way down the beach until I saw the crowd and saw his red bathing suit," Maggie tried to explain.

"And how long was it before you started looking for him?" Vickie asked with an accusing tone in her voice.

"Vickie, why don't you and Margaret sort this out later? I'm sure that Nick would like to see you now," Doc said as he led Vickie into the exam room.

"Hi, Mom!" Nicky said as Vickie walked into the room. "I drank some ocean."

"How do you feel, sweetheart? Are you ready to go home?" she asked her son.

"Yeah, I guess so. This bed isn't very comfortable, and I don't want them to give me any more shots. I don't like them," Nick announced.

"Can he leave now, Doc?" Vickie asked.

"How come you don't like my bed, Sport? I take my naps on it all of the time," Doc said to Nick as he was helping him sit up on the bed. "Here, I am going to give you this pair of hospital pants to wear. Your swim trunks are all wet. They are a little big for you, but we will roll them up and tie them tight around the waist so you won't be embarrassed by them slipping down."

Vickie helped her son put the pants on and tie them up, then led him out of the room, followed by Doctor Jansen. She gave Maggie a scathing look, and the three of them went out to the car.

Vickie looked at Maggie as they got into the car and said, "You and I will have our conversation later. Not a word now. Do you understand, Margaret?"

"Yes," Maggie answered. She knew that she was in for it. Her mother never called her Margaret unless she was really, really angry at her. And Maggie knew that her mother had cause to be angry with her. She had forgotten about Nicky. She was caught up in trying to impress some of the boys in her school and didn't even think about Nick being there. It wasn't until she realized that she hadn't put any of the sun lotion on him that she remembered that he was there with her.

But Nicky should have come and told her that he was going for a walk down the beach. He shouldn't have left like that.

# CHAPTER 2

*V*ickie made sure that Nicholas was settled in his bed and was comfortable. She wanted him to take a nap for about an hour; then he could go into the living room and watch TV. Superman would be on when he got up, and that was his favorite show.

Maggie had gone straight to her room when they got home from the clinic. She took a shower and changed into jeans and a tee shirt and was sitting on her bed when her mother came in.

"Explain to me what happened, Margaret," Vickie asked her daughter.

"He just walked off, Mom. He didn't tell me where he was going. I got the sunscreen out to rub on his back, arms, and legs and looked over, and he wasn't there," she explained.

"How long was it before you noticed that he was gone?" Vickie inquired.

"Just a few minutes. I was talking to some of the kids, looked over to where he was sitting on his towel, and noticed that his bag was gone too. He must have taken it with him. He had some idea that he could find sand dollars and sell them to gift stores for people to paint on. He said he was going to make all kinds of money that way," Maggie tried to explain.

"Maggie, tell me again, the truth this time. How long was it before you noticed that Nick was gone?" Vickie asked again.

"Honest, Mom. It was only a few minutes," Maggie said.

"Well, Nick said that he sat there for a long time with nothing to do. He said he walked over to you once, but you ignored him," Vickie explained to her.

"He did not come over to me, Mom. I did not see him," pleaded Maggie.

"You know what I think?" Vickie asked.

"What?" mumbled Maggie.

"I think you told Nick to sit there and be quiet and not bother you, and you forgot about him. And because of your negligence, we almost lost him. Because of the grace of God, two off-duty paramedics were at the beach today and were in the right place at the right time and saved his life," Vickie stated.

"For the time being, you are to stay in your room. When your dad gets home, he and I will talk, and we will decide what the consequences will be for your actions today. I am so disappointed in you, Margaret. All I asked you to do was to watch your little brother today, and you couldn't even do that for me," Vickie stated as she got up and left the room.

Maggie knew that she was in for some really serious punishment. Her dad didn't mess around. He had never hit her, but had come close a couple of times. He could get really worked up about things and then would explode. She just hoped that her punishment wouldn't mess up her whole summer. Maggie really wanted a boyfriend, and she wanted to get one this summer so she would be ready for her sophomore year in September. She wanted to walk down the hallways of her school on the arm of a neat-looking boy. If her parents made her punishment longer than a week, she would miss out on all of the activities that her friends had planned.

Vickie called her boss and told him what had happened with Nicholas. He was sympathetic and told Vickie to stay home with him. There were plenty of cashiers available, and she needed to be with her son.

Vickie was grateful to have the rest of the day off. She really wished she didn't have to work, but Dan's business wasn't doing as well as they had hoped. He worked so hard but wasn't able to get any new clients, and the price of logs has stayed pretty much even.

Victoria Mulligan was born in Eugene, Oregon. Her parents had just graduated from the University of Oregon. Her dad had a degree in accounting and had always wanted to live at the beach. Her mom was a teacher and got her first job teaching in the elementary school in Florence. Vickie was their only child and grew up in a household with all the love and attention poured on her that her parents could give. Unfortunately, they gave it all to her and forgot to give it to each other. Victoria was just starting school when they divorced, and her dad moved to Portland. He soon remarried and had another family, and Vickie was lucky to see him once a year. Her mother continued to teach in the Florence elementary school but was killed in a car accident two weeks before Vickie was to graduate from high school.

Because Vickie was 18 years old, she was on her own. She inherited the house and all of her mother's estate. She had been able to invest thirteen years of child support and some of her salary, and along with life insurance, Vickie had a pretty substantial inheritance. The house she lived in had no mortgage, and the only bills she had to pay were for utilities, taxes, and what food she ate.

All of the young men in town knew that Victoria Mulligan was a good catch, but she did not date. She was not interested in going out with anyone and didn't even attend her graduation ceremony. She had no one to invite. She sent an announcement to her dad, but he only sent a check for $100.00. Not even a note was included with the check. He had not contacted her in any way when her mother had been killed, so she knew he was totally out of the picture. When she turned 18 and he was able to stop sending child support, she was totally out of his life.

Vickie had a lot of girlfriends, and they all tried to get her to go out with them on the weekends, but she was not interested. She was in deep mourning for her mother and did not want to see anyone. She did start going to church. Her house was a block from the Florence Community Methodist Church. She was out walking one Sunday morning and heard the music coming from the open door. The sound of the organ playing drew her to the door. The service had started, and she just stood at the back of the church and listened. During a pause between the end of the first song and a prayer from the pastor, a gentleman came up to her and asked if she would like to be seated. Vickie shook her head and whispered that she would just stand there if it was okay. The gentleman nodded and stood next to her.

When the church service was over, the gentleman introduced himself as Daniel Roberts. He had been substituting for one of the regular ushers who was ill today. "Would you like to go into the parlor for a cup of coffee or juice? We have a social time every Sunday after the service, and you are most welcome," Daniel asked her.

"No, I am not dressed for it, and anyway, I just heard the music and stopped to listen. I need to get home now," Vickie answered.

As she turned around again, Dan called out to her, "Come again. We would love to have you join us."

The next Sunday, Vickie dressed properly for church and walked the short distance to attend the service. She sat in the back of the sanctuary and loved the music and the message that was given that morning. The message was about forgiveness and how God would forgive us all for our sins if we believed in Him.

Forgiveness was something that Vickie had a hard time with. She could not forgive her father for abandoning her and her mother when she was a little girl, and she could not forgive the drunk man who ran his car into her mother's and caused her death. Both events had deprived her of the family she so craved.

She began to look forward to Sunday mornings when she could dress in nice clothes and go to church. She was beginning to know some of the people who attended and was interacting with them at the social time after the service. And it seemed that Dan Roberts was always close by to introduce her to someone new.

He was standing close to her one Sunday after church when all of a sudden he asked, "Vickie, would you like to go with me for a quick bite to eat after we are done here?"

"Yeah, that would be nice. I was late this morning and didn't have time to eat breakfast, and I am hungry. Thanks," Vickie answered him.

"Do you like Mo's?" Dan asked.

"Who doesn't like Mo's! I am so glad they opened one here. Now I don't have to go all the way to Newport or Lincoln City to get a good cup of chowder."

"Do you want to drive your car home and have me pick you up there?" Dan asked her.

"Oh! No, I walk. I just live a couple of blocks away. I very rarely take the car out. I walk most of where I need to go," Vickie answered him.

"Okay! Shall we go now before the line gets so long outside the restaurant that it will be dinner time before we eat?" he asked.

Vickie laughed and followed him out of the church and down the stairs to his car. It was parked in the parking lot. There were still a lot of cars in the lot. "It looks like the congregation is talkative this morning. They are probably talking about you and me leaving together," Dan laughed.

Vickie didn't laugh. She didn't want people talking about her. There had been enough talk after her mother was killed. Everyone was trying to tell her what to do, and she was tired of it all. She was old enough to do as she pleased now.

Vickie was quiet all the way over to Mo's. There were only a couple of people waiting for tables. "We lucked out," Dan said. "We got here before the huge Sunday crowd."

They each ordered a bowl of chowder. Vickie only wanted a glass of water with hers, and Dan ordered a Coke. They ate for a while in silence, then Dan put down his spoon and asked, "Did I say something wrong? You have said very little since we left church."

"No, you didn't say something wrong. It's just that I don't like the idea of people talking about me. I had enough of that growing up and after my mother was killed. It seems like I was known as 'Poor Victoria,' and have been all of my life. When my father left us, it was 'Poor Victoria, she has to live without a father.' Then after Mama was killed, it was 'Poor Victoria, she has to live without a mother now.' It does get very tiring, and it seems that people do not want me to control my own life. I am 18, almost 19, and doing fine.

"Do you have a job, Vickie, or something to keep you busy?" Dan asked.

"No! I haven't found anything that I really want to do. I don't want to go away to school. I hate the idea of renting out my house to someone I don't know, and I would have to put all of my stuff into storage if I did. That would be a monthly expense I don't need. I suppose I could take some correspondence courses, but I don't know what I want to do. Fortunately, I do not have to work to get by. I am able to live comfortably on what I get each month from Social

Security survivor benefits and an annuity that my mom set up for me years ago," Vickie explained. "You know, you are the first one that I have said anything to about the way I live, except for my banker and financial advisor," Vickie commented.

"I'm honored that you would trust me," Dan said. "Do you date, Vickie?"

"No. Most of the men only want two things: sex and my money. I am unwilling to give them either," Vickie stated firmly.

Dan smiled and said, "Good for you!"

When they had finished their meal, they left and went back out to Dan's car. "Would you like to walk along the beach? It's fairly early yet, or do you have something else you need to do?"

"No, I don't, and I would love a walk on the beach," Vickie answered.

That first walk on the beach became a regular habit on Sunday afternoons. They also became regulars at Mo's on Sundays after church. After about a month, they were noticed holding hands as they walked, and people noticed that oftentimes, Dan had his hand on Vickie's back as he led her down the stairs and to his car after church. They all knew that something was happening with them, but no one said a word to either of them.

Vickie seemed to be opening up more. She was more animated while she was talking to people. She joined the church choir and was faithful about attending rehearsals every Thursday evening. Dan had convinced her to drive to the church when she was going to be there in the evenings. He did not want her walking home in the dark. She joined a Wednesday afternoon Bible study group and was fascinated by what she was learning.

After six months of having lunch with him and walking on the beach, Vickie finally invited Dan to her home for a meal. He appeared with a bouquet of flowers and a bottle of sparkling cider. Neither one of them drank any alcohol, and sparkling cider was the closest thing to champagne that Dan could think of. Vickie was a very good cook but had a limited number of dishes that she could cook well. Spaghetti was one of them. She made a big pot of spaghetti with garlic bread and a tossed salad to go with it. Dan ate until he was ready to bust and could not say enough good things about the meal.

They talked that evening for a long time. Dan opened up about his childhood, schooling, and working at his father's lumber yard. He would take over the business someday and had learned it from the bottom up. He had worked in the forest cutting trees, loading them on trucks, hauling them to the yard, and stacking them in the proper piles according to type and grade of the logs. He was now working the loader, putting the logs on the trucks to ship out to the mills. In what spare time he had, he was learning the business end of the job. His dad had done a good job of building Roberts Lumber into a successful business, and Dan was proud to be working for his dad. He admired him for his efforts. Dan's mom had died when he was a small boy, and his dad had raised him on his own. He did remarry when Dan was in the 7th grade, but that did not last, and they had been on their own ever since.

When Dan left that evening, he gave Vickie a hug and thanked her for a great meal and the container of leftover spaghetti that he was carrying out with him. "My dad is going to love this. He's a pretty good cook, but this will be a real treat for him."

Vickie was becoming very attracted to Dan Roberts. It was now she wanted her mother the most. She wanted someone to talk to and ask questions about all of these emotions that she was having about Dan. Her mother had been gone a year now, and the feeling of loss had not lessened at all. She missed her more now than when she first was killed. There was no one that she could talk to.

# CHAPTER 3

The next Sunday, the message that Rev. Silas gave was about love and marriage. It being June and the wedding season, that seemed to be an appropriate time for this particular sermon.

Vickie was sitting next to Dan, as usual, and she was listening to the sermon very intently. As the sermon continued, she thought that maybe the reverend was someone she could talk to. He wasn't a female, but because of his profession, she thought that maybe he would understand some of the feelings that she had. Maybe she would call and make an appointment with him.

Vickie and Dan went on their usual trek to Mo's for clam chowder and their walk on the beach that day, but Vickie was very quiet.

"Something wrong, Vick?" Dan asked with concern.

"No, I am just in a quiet mood today. This week is the first anniversary of Mama's accident. I need to go to the cemetery later on this afternoon," Vickie explained.

"Oh, honey, I am sorry. I didn't know!" Dan said as he put his arm around her shoulder. "Do you want me to come with you?"

"No!" Vickie answered very quickly. "This is something I have to do by myself. I do go there fairly often, but this is a special time."

"I had best get home, so it is not too late by the time I get home. The cemetery where she is buried is about 5 miles out of town. She had all of the arrangements made long before she was killed. I guess she was protecting me from having to make those decisions. She had no way of knowing it would be sooner than later, though," Vickie said thoughtfully.

Vickie thanked Dan for the lunch and jumped out of his car before he could get out and escort her to the door. "See you later," she hollered.

Dan was surprised at her reaction but watched her go into her house and drove slowly away.

Vickie quickly changed her clothes and grabbed her purse and car keys and left for the cemetery. She was in a hurry to talk to her mother. She knew that her mother couldn't answer her questions, but at least she would be able to pour out her thoughts and feelings to her.

Unbeknownst to Vickie, Dan had decided to follow her to the cemetery. He did not want to intrude on her time there but wanted to make sure that she was okay. He was worried about her. When she parked her car and walked toward her mother's grave, he parked down the lane and walked parallel to her so that she could not see him. He saw her fall down on her knees in front of the headstone, put some flowers on the grave, and start to cry. All Dan wanted to do was go over and hold her in his arms, but he knew that he couldn't let her know that he was there. He was afraid of losing her, and he loved her so much; he didn't want to hurt her in any way.

That day, Vickie poured all of the confusion and feelings she had for Dan Roberts out to her mother. She cried for the loss of her mama and for the love she was feeling for Dan and the fact that her mama could not rejoice with her in this feeling.

Dan heard it all. He was both happy and sad—happy that Vickie felt the same way he did and profoundly sad that she could not share the feeling with her mother. He felt the same way about his mother, but at least he had his dad to talk to. Vickie had no one.

When Dan came home from work the evening of Nicky's accident, he was tired, hungry, and cranky because he could not get his truck fixed in time to make the delivery he needed to make to the mill.

When he walked in the back door, he knew that something was wrong the minute he saw Vickie's face. "What happened?" he asked with concern. He could tell Vickie had been crying. Her beautiful face, which usually greeted him with a smile, was streaked with tears.

"Nicky had an accident today," she said.

"What kind of an accident? Did he break a bone or something?" Dan asked.

"No! He almost died," she explained.

"What! What happened? Is he okay? Is he home?" Dan demanded loudly.

"Yes to all. He was at the beach and was apparently either pulled out by an undertow or hit by a big wave and was pulled out into the water. The tide pushed him back into shore. Thank God a couple of off-duty paramedics were right there and got him breathing again and rushed him to the clinic and Doc Jensen. He is okay, Dan. He is in his room resting right now. Doc gave him a very mild sedative so that he would remain calm and quiet for a time," Vickie explained as calmly as she could.

"Where was Maggie?" Dan asked ominously.

"She was there on the beach with some of her friends. She says that he walked away and didn't tell her where he was going. I had asked her to watch him just before I left for work. She didn't like it, but said that she would. I asked her how long it was before she realized he was gone, and she said it was just a few minutes. She had forgotten to put the sunscreen on him and went to get him, and he wasn't where he had put his towel. She apparently walked down the beach until she saw a crowd, went over to investigate, and saw his red bathing suit.

To tell you the truth, I don't know whether to believe her or not. She was really keen on being with her friends today to celebrate the end of the school year and didn't want to watch Nick, but she says that it was just a couple of minutes before she realized he was gone. I have not had a chance to ask Nick. He was too groggy," Vickie finished the explanation.

Dan sat down at the kitchen table with his hands covering his face. To think that he almost lost his son was unthinkable. Losing either one of his children would be more than he could take.

"I told Maggie that we would talk about whatever punishment she should get. Honestly, Dan, I don't believe that it was just a few minutes before she noticed that he was gone. I think it was a lot longer than that, and Nicky just got bored and decided to go for a walk. I know he understands that he is not to go off on his own, especially near the water, but I also know that Maggie was not looking after him the way she was supposed to. I don't know what to do!" Vickie said in frustration.

"Why did Maggie have to watch him? Isn't he usually with Beth?" Dan asked.

"Beth called this morning. She is sick, running a fever and throwing up. She sent Josh to his grandma in Eugene," Vickie explained.

Dan got up from the chair and walked over to the sink where Vickie was standing and gave her a big hug. "I know working is hard on you, honey, and I know all of your mama's money is sitting there in the bank and in investments, but we did say we wouldn't use any of it to live on; that we would save it for the kids' educations. If I didn't have to plow so much back into the business, we would be in a situation where you didn't have to work, and we wouldn't have to think about using your inheritance."

"I know, Dan, but I grew up as a latch-key kid, and I swore I would always be home for my kids. At least I work the day shift and don't have to be gone from you and the kids at night," Vickie murmured into Dan's shoulder.

He gave her one more squeeze and said, "I guess I had better talk to our teenage daughter. No one said raising a girl would be easy," he said as he gave her a pat on the backside.

Maggie had heard her dad come home, so she was expecting him to come to her room sooner or later. She heard him knock on the door and ask to come in. "Okay," she said quietly.

Dan walked into his daughter's bedroom, looked around, and said, "Do you ever clean your room? It is really a mess in here."

"Mama says that too. I know where almost everything is, though," Maggie answered in defense of her decorating style.

"Why don't you tell me what happened today with Nick, from the beginning, please?" Dan asked his daughter.

"Mama asked me to watch him today because Mrs. Freeman is sick. Dad, I had already made plans with my friends to meet at the beach this morning to celebrate the end of the school year. Sometimes Nick can be such a pest, and I didn't want to watch him, but I took him to the beach with me. He put his towel down and sat on the sand playing with some kind of toy he had brought with him. I walked over to my friends, who were just a short distance away. A few minutes later, I reached into my bag for something and discovered the bottle of sunscreen there and realized that I had forgotten to put any on Nick. I took the bottle and walked over to where he was, but he was gone. I asked some of my friends if they had seen him, and they said that they hadn't, so I started walking down the beach looking for him. He was wearing a red swimsuit, so I thought that I would find him pretty easily. I saw the crowd down the beach and went toward it, thinking that maybe Nick was there watching something. Then I saw Nick lying on his side on the sand and throwing up water. I knelt down beside him, calling to him, but all he did was throw up seawater. The paramedic told me what had happened. I told him where the clinic was and ran to the store to tell Mama."

"Tell me again how long it was before you noticed that Nick was not sitting near your group," Dan asked Maggie.

"I told you, Daddy, that it was just a few minutes," she answered.

"Maggie! Tell me the truth. I know that every time you call me Daddy now, you either want something or you are not telling me the honest truth," Dan said.

Maggie sat there for a few minutes wondering how she was going to get out of this and finally realized that she was not going to get out of it. Nicky almost died because she was not watching him properly. "It was probably more like 30 to 40 minutes," she mumbled very quietly.

"Maggie, you know that Nick is a special child and has needs that a lot of other children don't have. We don't talk about it often, but Nick is slightly retarded, and he needs to be supervised all of the time. He doesn't have the judgment that other young boys have at age 10," Dan was trying to explain to her.

"I know that, Dad, but sometimes he can be such a pest. I just wanted to be with my friends," Maggie said.

"How often in the last few months has your mom asked you to watch Nicky on a Saturday?" Dan asked.

"None," Maggie answered quietly.

"One Saturday every few months isn't going to ruin your social life, Maggie. Do you know why your mother is working? She is working so that you can have nice clothes and school supplies and go to movies with your friends. She is working so that both you and Nick can have a better life, and right now she is learning a whole new system of doing her job, and she is scared to death that if she doesn't learn it, she will be demoted and make less money, or she will be outright fired. I think that you can take care of your little brother once in a while, and your social life will survive," Dan firmly stated. "And Margaret, do not ever lie to either your mother or me again."

# CHAPTER 4

---·•·◆·•·---

*D*an walked into Nick's bedroom to find Vickie there sitting on the edge of Nick's bed talking about sand dollars.

"Hi, Sport! I understand you got a little wet today," Dan said in a joking manner, but thankful to God that his son was lying there safe and sound.

"Yeah, Dad! I was looking for sand dollars. I saw some once when Mama and I went into a store, and they were all painted up and looked real pretty. I thought that if I could find some, I could sell them to the store and make some money," Nicky said, explaining what he was doing on the beach.

"Where was Maggie? Did she go with you to try to find the sand dollars?" Vickie asked.

"No. She was too busy making googly eyes at some older guy in her school. I went by myself," Nick explained.

"You know you are not supposed to go off on your own, don't you?" Vickie asked.

"I know, Mom, but there was nothing to do, and I was bored. Anyway, I thought that I would make some money for us so we could go out and get a hamburger," Nick said very simply.

"Okay, Sport. You get some rest. Do you want the TV on?" Dan asked.

"Thanks, Dad. I like having a TV in my room. Sometimes I get tired of watching all those shows you and Mom watch," Nick commented as he laid his head back on his pillow to watch his favorite TV show.

Maggie knew she had to get some dinner ready for her family, but she was exhausted and really didn't want to cook. Dan could see that she was about on her last leg and suggested that he go to the hamburger stand and get dinner for all of them. Big, juicy hamburgers, French fries, and milkshakes were in order for the evening's meal.

"You are the absolute best, do you know that?" Vickie commented as she went up to her husband, gave him a hug, and a big kiss smack on the mouth.

"Maybe hamburgers for the kids, and you and I can retire to the bedroom for the night," he teased her.

"Nothing doing! I want one of those hamburgers. I'm starved. I didn't get my lunch break. In fact, it is still sitting in the refrigerator in the break room at work," Vickie commented as she wiggled out of his embrace to clean off the table for dinner. "You go get the burgers, and I will make some chocolate pudding for dessert."

Dan came home with the burgers, fries, and milkshakes, and everyone gathered for their meal at the kitchen table. As usual, Nicky said grace before they ate. Maggie was especially quiet during the meal. Nick was still taken with the idea of finding sand dollars and selling them to the store. He was busy explaining that they had to be perfect, though. They could not be broken or cracked at all.

Maggie was watching her brother closely during dinner. She marveled at the fact that he made no mention of the fact that he almost died that day. Maybe he didn't realize how close he was. Thank God for those two paramedics being on the beach at that particular time. The outcome would have been so much different if they hadn't been there.

Maggie also wondered what her punishment would be. She hoped that it wouldn't louse up her plans for the summer too much.

When dinner was over, Vickie went to give Nicky a bath and get him settled back into bed. He loved his bath time, so he didn't object to the idea at all.

"Maggie, you stay here and help me clean up," Dan said as Maggie was about ready to leave the kitchen for her bedroom. "I want to talk to you. Your mom and I have decided what the consequences of your actions will be today. You will stay home on Saturdays and take care of Nicky while your mother and I are at work. You will fix him lunch and make sure that he is safe."

"But Dad, that is the only day that a lot of my friends can get together. They have to work during the week and can't get away," Maggie cried. "How long will I have to do this?"

"Every Saturday for three months, Maggie," Dan answered her.

"No! Every Saturday? That is not fair. It will ruin my whole summer," Maggie stated angrily.

"Maggie, your whole life could have been ruined today. You were very lucky that those two paramedics were on the beach today. Nicky could have died. Then how would you have felt? A few Saturdays spent with your brother will not kill you. It might make you a better person. You may leave and go to your room now if you wish."

Maggie stomped off to her room mumbling something about her entire life being ruined. Dan just smiled. Little did she know that her life was just starting. She was only 14 years old. She had a lot of life ahead of her, God willing.

Maggie so wished she had a phone in her room. She wanted to call Jeannie, her best friend. Jeannie could give her some good advice on how to get out of her Saturday "babysitting" job. She could not believe that her parents would make her stay home with Nick every

Saturday for the whole summer. She plopped down on her bed and wondered what she was going to do.

After getting Nicky settled in bed happily watching his shows on TV, Vickie went into the living room to sit with Dan. He was reading the newspaper. The Portland Oregonian and the Eugene Register-Guard were both delivered to them, and Vickie always picked up a copy of the weekly Siuslaw News, the local paper for Florence and Lane County. A stack of them was delivered to the store every week. It was a lot to read, but both Dan and Vickie liked to keep up with what was going on in the world, and it seemed that the papers were the easiest way to do it. Neither one of them had the time to sit in front of the TV and listen to the newscasters drone on, and Dan felt that so many times, they repeated themselves over and over again.

Vickie had taught herself how to sew when she was in high school. Her mother had encouraged her and bought her the best equipment she could at the time. It gave her great pleasure to produce a garment for either Maggie or herself that looked like it was purchased in a fancy department store. Twice a year, once just before school started and once in the spring, Vickie and Maggie would make a trip to Portland. The big department store there, Meier and Frank, would have a fashion show, and they would go and look at all of the new designs and fashion trends. Then they would go to the fabric store and look at all of the pattern books. Vickie was very good at putting different patterns together to get the look of the new designs. Then off to the fabric section of the store to pick out the material needed to make the new clothes.

Maggie loved the trips to Portland. Just she and her mom would go, and they would have a great time. They would usually take in one of the new movies at the big theaters in downtown Portland.

Only Jeannie, Maggie's best friend, knew that her clothes were homemade. Everyone else thought that she bought them in either Eugene or through a catalog. There was always something about the garment that was just a little different or unique that would set it apart from anybody else's clothes. Maggie loved the comments she would get from the girls at school. She felt that she was one of the best-dressed girls at school her freshman year.

Now, she wondered if she and her mom would make the trip to Portland before school started. Would that highlight of her summer be ruined too?

Sunday morning was a busy one in the Roberts' household. They were all up and getting ready for church. Vickie had to be there early because she sang in the choir, and they had a quick rehearsal before the 11:00 AM service. Nick was not able to sit still during the whole service, so he was taken down to the Sunday School area along with several other young children to play while the message was being read. Dan and Maggie sat in the congregation during the entire service. Sometimes Dan served as an usher and passed the collection plates, but not every Sunday. This particular Sunday, he sat with Maggie. He was sure that people knew about Nick's accident yesterday, and he also knew that there would be talk. He wanted everyone to know that he stood behind his daughter and that she was not going to be hung out to dry.

As soon as the service was over, Nick came bounding up the stairs with a picture in his hand for Maggie. "I made this for you, Maggie," Nick said with great pride. "It is a picture of a sand dollar, all painted pretty."

Maggie took the picture, looked at it, and said to Nicky, "Nick, that is the best present I have ever received from you. I am going to take it home and put it on the wall in my room. Thank you so much," she said as she bent down and gave him a hug.

"Dad, I would have made one for you too, but I ran out of time," Nick announced to his father.

"That's okay, Sport. You really did a good job on that one for Maggie," Dan said with some emotion in his voice.

Vickie came walking out of the choir room, saw her family standing there waiting for her, and gave them a great big smile.

"Mom, look at the picture I painted for Maggie. Do you like it?" Nick asked his mom.

Vickie looked at Maggie and saw that she had some tears in her eyes. Maggie held the picture out for her to see. "Nicky, that is one of the prettiest pictures I have ever seen. That was very nice of you to paint it for Maggie," she said.

Nick bounded out of the church and down the steps headed toward the car, hollering back to his family, "She had a hard day yesterday, Mom; she deserves something pretty."

Nicholas Roberts' whole family, plus several people who were standing near them, had tears running down their cheeks when they heard that.

# CHAPTER 5

The summer started out very poorly for Maggie Roberts. She so wanted to be with her friends at the beach on Saturday, but her punishment for not watching Nicky properly was to watch him every Saturday for the entire summer.

She soon discovered that Nick was not so bad to be around. They would get up very early in the morning and go out onto the beach at first light to find sand dollars and other shells that were not broken. A couple of times, they found glass floats at the edge of the waterline. Maggie would go in after those. She wouldn't let Nick near the water. She finally started making him wear a life jacket. He didn't want to, but Maggie insisted.

"Nick, if one of those strange waves came up and grabbed you into the water, I would not be able to get you out. And there probably wouldn't be any paramedics on the beach at this hour of the morning. So, a life jacket it is!" Maggie insisted.

"Okay, Maggie. I don't want you to worry," Nick answered.

When they had gathered 20 or so sand dollars, Maggie showed Nicky how to wash them and get all of the sand out of them, then lay them on the deck rail to dry. After they were good and dry, Maggie sealed them with some special sealer, then she and Nicky started painting them. On nice days, they worked on the table on the deck. Maggie was surprised at how good Nicky was at painting the shells. He had a real eye for putting colors together, and his designs were unique.

Maggie realized that she was having a really good time on her Saturdays with Nicky. She looked forward to spending the time with him. Jeannie, her best friend, would call and want to talk about what occurred at the beach that day, but Maggie realized that she really didn't care. Her time with Nicky was much more fun and productive.

One Saturday in the middle of July, Nicky and Maggie were coming back from the beach with their bags full of shells and a few sand dollars when the ground started shaking. It was just a little shake and didn't last long, but Maggie looked at Nicky in surprise.

"Do you think that was an earthquake?" she asked.

"I've heard about them, but never felt one. I don't know. I watched part of a movie about a very large earthquake once. Buildings were falling down and people were dying. I wasn't supposed to be watching it, and I turned it off because it scared me, but that's all I know about earthquakes," Nicky answered his sister.

Nicky just trotted on, and Maggie followed, but she was a little concerned. She had heard that sometimes earthquakes could cause tidal waves, and those could be bad. She urged Nicky on home because she wanted to call her mom and see if she should be doing anything to take care of the house. They were a few blocks off of the street, but maybe if a tidal wave was bad, it would come that far. The IGA grocery store was closer to the ocean than their house.

When Maggie and Nicky got back to their house, the phone was ringing. Maggie answered it, and it was her mother calling. "Maggie, I want you to listen to me very carefully. Please go into my bedroom and get the suitcases that are on the top of my closet shelf. Take one for you and one for Nick. Pack enough clothes for three or four days for both you and Nick and put the suitcases by the door to the garage. Then, get the cooler out of the garage and take it into the kitchen and put as much food from the refrigerator and freezer in it that you can fit. Grab milk, sandwich meat, eggs, and all of the essentials. You know what they are. I will be home in a few minutes to pack some things for Daddy and me and get some papers that we will need. Please do not scare Nick. Make a game of it if you can. Thanks, honey. I will see you in a few minutes," Vickie explained to her.

Maggie hung up the phone and explained to Nick that Mom and Dad decided to go on a short camping trip. Dad needed some downtime, and he was going to check out some stands of trees and decided to take them all along with him. She prompted him to go pack some of his clothes, underwear, socks, jeans, and pajamas. Nicky thought that was a great idea and went to get his clothes out of his drawers right away.

Maggie was scared but did exactly what her mother had told her to do. Vickie came in the back door just as Maggie was finishing up filling the cooler. Maggie looked at her mom and asked, "Is it going to be bad, Mama?"

"It could be, sweetheart. Where's Nick?" she asked.

"He is packing his clothes. I told him to put what you said in the suitcase, but I don't know what else he has. I will go check on him," Maggie announced.

"Thanks, Maggie!" Vickie said as she headed for her bedroom to get clothes for herself and Dan and to pick up their file of important papers.

"Hi, Mom!" Nick said as he walked into his mother's room. "This is going to be fun. I love to go camping. Are we going to meet Dad at the lumber yard?"

"We are, honey. He will be waiting for us there. He is anxious to get started on this trip," Vickie explained to him.

Maggie was busy putting things into the trunk of Vickie's car. She had several bags of groceries from the pantry cupboard too and picked up the picnic basket that they had on the floor of the pantry. That had plates, cups, silverware, and cooking utensils in it for their camping trips. She also grabbed a can opener out of the drawer. She had packed several cans of soup.

"Mom, can I take some of my sand dollars to work on?" Nick asked his mother.

"Honey, I don't think you are going to have time on this trip. There will be so many other things for us to do. Maybe you will be able to find some other things to paint," Vickie said, trying to be as sensitive as she could to Nick's feelings.

Maggie and Nick piled into the car along with all of the other stuff, and Vickie left the driveway, looking at the house she had lived in since she was a little girl and hoping that it would still be standing when she saw it again. Dan had called her and told her that there were reports of a very strong earthquake out to sea, and it could cause a major tsunami along the Oregon Coast. The government was just beginning to form evacuation routes along the coast, but there were not a lot of signs up yet, and people didn't know too much about them. Dan was aware of the routes because he ran a business that had vehicles on the roads all of the time. If a wave hit and his trucks were damaged and blocked the exit routes, it could cause a major problem getting people to safety. They were large trucks and carried very large logs that could cause roads to be blocked.

Dan's parents had left him a cabin up in the coastal mountains. Dan had made a trip up there a few weeks ago just to check it out and see if he needed to do any repairs. There was no running water, but it had a pump in the kitchen area. The roof looked good, and the outhouse was still in one piece. Vickie and Maggie didn't like having to use it, but it was all they had. There was a large fireplace along with a good wood stove. Vickie had become very adept at cooking meals on the wood stove. They had spent a lot of romantic weekends up here before Maggie was born. Dan swore that Maggie was conceived at the cabin.

Vickie, Maggie, and Nick arrived at the lumber yard within a half hour of leaving home. Vickie had stopped at the bank to withdraw some money from their savings account. She wanted to have enough cash on hand in case she needed it.

Dan had decided that they would take one of his large pickup trucks. They had a small back seat that Maggie and Nick could sit in, and they had a cover over the bed of the truck. All of their stuff would be covered from the elements that way. He had some tools that he wanted to take with him.

He gave Vickie a hug and asked, "Are you and the kids okay?"

"Maggie is scared, but she was super about gathering everything together. She even remembered some things that I had forgotten about. Nick is just excited about going on an unexpected camping trip. He doesn't know that we are going to the cabin. He wanted to bring his sand dollars, but I discouraged that by telling him that maybe he could find something else to paint," Vickie explained.

Maggie was busy getting the groceries transferred to the pickup, and Nick had gone into the office to say hello to some of the men who worked there. He loved the lumber yard, and all of the employees loved him.

They all piled into the truck to leave the yard. Dan had the radio on low so he could hear any reports about a possible tsunami. There had been a report about 15 minutes before that another aftershock had occurred, which made the possibility of a huge wave even greater. Both Dan and Vickie were just hoping it would not reach their street. Unfortunately, Front Street and the ones just behind it could be devastated. The grocery store would be a building that would go quickly.

In the past, there had been a few waves that were high enough to almost reach Front Street, but they never went over the wall. Both Dan and Vickie remembered a couple of incidents where waves threatened the businesses along the street, but the high wall always saved them.

"Dad, how come you decided to go to the cabin now? I thought you and I were going to go there when Mom and Maggie went to Portland?" Nicky asked.

"We will probably go up then, Nick, but I just wanted to spend some time with my family. We don't have a chance to spend a lot of time together like this. Both Mom and I are so busy working, and you are busy gathering and painting your sand dollars. I just wanted some time with you," Dan explained.

"Thanks, Dad!" Nicky answered. "It will be fun."

Vickie thanked God that he was oblivious to all of the concern and worry. She wished she could make it the same for Maggie.

There was heavier than usual traffic heading east on Highway 126. It seemed that a lot of people were taking heed of the tsunami warnings and getting away from the coast. In about three miles, they would turn left onto a side road and up into the mountains towards their cabin and, they hoped, safety.

When they finally reached the dirt road that led to their cabin, both Vickie and Dan breathed a sigh of relief. They were always grateful when they reached this spot because they knew that safety and a warm place to stay were just ahead of them. When Dan stopped the truck, Nick scampered out and ran around, happy to be out of the confines of a seat belt, but also happy to be in one of his favorite places.

"Hurry, Dad. Unlock the door. I want to see if everything is the same," Nick begged his father.

"Just a minute, Sport. I have to get the key out of my pocket," he explained to Nick. He opened the door, and Nick ran in to check the condition of the inside of the cabin. He soon pronounced everything okay and safe for them to unpack the truck and move in.

Maggie was very quiet as she carried sacks of groceries into the cabin. She loved being here but was worried about all of her friends at home. She hadn't called anyone to let them know where she was going. Jeannie was going to worry, and now there was no way to let her know where they were. They had to drive down to the highway to reach the gas station and a phone. She just hoped that Jeannie would be okay and that her parents had listened to the news of a possible big wave doing damage to their city.

Maggie and Nicky shared a bedroom while they were at the cabin. They always left the door open so that the heat from the large fireplace could keep them warm at night. Even in the summer, it got cold up in the mountains. They had nice warm sleeping bags and blankets to cover them, but without the fire, they would get cold. As Maggie was unpacking some of her things and putting them away, she unpacked her picture of the sand dollar and propped it up against the mirror of the dresser.

"Gee, Maggie. You brought your sand dollar?" Nicky asked with surprise.

"Sure. That goes everywhere with me now. It is my most treasured possession," Maggie answered.

Nicky looked at his sister in awe and gave her a big hug around the waist. Vickie was standing in the doorway watching the exchange between her children and was amazed at the change in her daughter in just a month. She was so worried about her home, her friends, and her city, but so proud of her children.

———— ✦ • ✦ • ◆ • ✦ • ✦ ————

# CHAPTER 6

One of the first things that Dan did when they got to the cabin was make sure the wood box was filled. They needed wood for both the fireplace and the cook stove. Nick always helped fill the wood bucket beside the stove. He knew that those pieces needed to be small enough to fit into the firebox. Dan would take care of the bigger logs needed for the fireplace. Vickie would make sure that the stove fire was started and get a large kettle of water on the stove to heat. Since there was no running water, they had to heat their water on the stove. They all learned to be sparing in their use of the water.

When they turned off the highway to head toward the cabin road, Dan stopped at the gas station and bought two large blocks of ice to keep their food cold. He had a large, insulated box just outside the back door of the cabin that served as their refrigerator. If need be, he could always go down to the station and get more ice, but he was hoping that the two blocks would last for the time they would have to stay there. Fortunately, he still got radio reception on his truck radio and was able to keep updated on what was happening in town.

"Maggie, you did a great job of picking food to bring. It was genius to bring the leftover spaghetti. It was an easy meal to fix for this first night here. Thanks!" Vickie praised her daughter.

"It was really good too, Mom," Nicky added with a big grin on his spaghetti-covered face.

"Time for our wild animal talk," Dan said.

"Dad, you say the same thing every time you come here," Nick said.

"I want you to make sure you understand, Nick. Do not ever go away from this cabin by yourself. You too, Maggie. The bears can be very aggressive, and there are other smaller animals that can hurt you also. We are the intruders here. This is their territory, and we have to respect the fact that we are just visiting here, so be very careful. When we go for walks, we lock up the cabin, and all four of us go together. Understood?" Dan asked.

"Yes, Dad!" Maggie answered.

"Yes, Dad!" Nick answered. "When can we go for a walk?"

"Have you looked outside, Nick? It is dark out there. It's almost bedtime. Come on, Nick, we will walk out to the outhouse, then come in, and you can get your pajamas on. How about a story before bed?" Dan asked.

"Dad, can I tell the story tonight?" Maggie asked.

Dan looked at her and said, "Sure, Maggie, but nothing scary."

"No, it's not a bit scary," Maggie replied.

As soon as things were cleaned up and all of the food stowed in its proper place, everyone got ready for bed. Before Dan got ready for bed, he made one more trip to the truck to listen to the news broadcast on the radio. So far, nothing had been reported about any damage along the coast, but the warning was still in effect.

The cabin did have electricity, and there was a bedside lamp beside Dan and Vickie's bed. Everyone crawled into their beds and waited for Maggie to start her story.

"This is a story about the sand dollar," Maggie started.

"Wow! There is a story about a sand dollar?" Nick asked in wonder.

"Yes, there is. I have been doing some research since you and I started looking for them. Did you know that the sand dollar used to be a living thing?" she asked.

Nick shook his head no.

"Well, the sand dollar lives on the bottom of the ocean. It is not white like it is when we find it. We are finding only the shell. When it is in the ocean, it is either a purple color or a brownish red. It is all covered in fuzz, kind of like hair all over it. It creeps along the bottom of the ocean, eating little bits of things off of the sandy and rocky bottom. When we find the shell on the sand, the living part of it has died and gone out of the shell. You know, Nick, if we ever find a sand dollar that is still brownish red and has fuzz on it, we need to very carefully put it back into the water. It is still alive and maybe can continue to live for a while longer if we return it to the sea. The sand dollar can live up to 10 years in the water. That is as old as you are, Nick."

Nicky's eyes were wide with wonder.

Maggie continued her story. "There are several legends about the sand dollar, but the one I like the most is that it reminds people of the story of Jesus. It is said that the five slits on the top represent the wounds of Jesus, and the star shape represents the Star of Bethlehem. The underside of the sand dollar reminds people of a poinsettia. Nick, that is the red plant that Dad gives to Mom every Christmas. The legend says that when you break open a sand dollar, the five jaws that the sand dollar eats with when it is alive remind people of doves. Remember, at Christmas, we see pictures of white doves on cards all of the time. When the sand dollar is broken open, it releases peace and goodwill in the world.

But that is only when it is broken naturally in the water. If we find a sand dollar on the beach, and it is whole and not cracked, we should keep it that way."

Maggie continued, "There are some other legends about the sand dollar, but this is the one I liked the best and the one I want to believe. The end."

"Wow!" Nick said again. "I guess we are lucky to find our sand dollars. I am sorry they died though," he said with concern.

Dan continued, "They get old too, just like people do, and sometimes they die. That happens to every living thing. Did you know that trees even get old? That is why I cut a lot of them down. They are getting old, and if I cut them at just the right time, the wood can be used for other things."

"Yeah, like houses and things," Nick added.

"That's right, and now it is time to crawl into your own bed. It is dark outside, and morning will come pretty fast if you don't get any sleep," Vickie announced.

Both Nicky and Maggie crawled into their sleeping bags, and Dan spread blankets over both of them. "Good night. I love you both."

"Love you too, Dad and Mom," Nick and Maggie said in unison.

Early the next morning, Dan went out to the truck to listen to the latest news on the radio. He heard that at about 1:00 AM, the tsunami hit the Oregon Coast, decimating several small cities and doing some serious damage to the cities along the middle of the coastline. The northern and southern coastlines had some pretty high tidal surges, but no damage to the cities proper, just a lot of debris deposited on the beach area. But the central coast had some major damage to cities. Lincoln City had major damage along Highway 101, which ran right through the city. There was significant damage to the boat docks in Newport, and the partially finished aquarium was severely damaged, along with some businesses along the coastline. The authorities were asking anyone with equipment or the means to help remove large pieces of debris from the cities and roads to please come to a central staging area to help.

Vickie was stoking the fire in the stove when Dan came back into the cabin. The kids were just beginning to stir in their room.

"What's the news?" Vickie asked with trepidation.

"It hit!" he said and proceeded to tell her what he had heard on the radio. "I don't know if it got as far as the house or not, but we have to get back. They are calling for anyone who has equipment that can move big logs and objects from the streets and the beach area. I have that equipment, and I need to get there to help. I would imagine the store is damaged, and they will probably need you there. If the house is okay, the kids can stay there; if it is damaged, they can stay at the church. They did announce that churches would be open as rescue centers, and the clinic was open for injured people to go to. Let's eat, pack up, and go home," Dan said. "If we had another vehicle here, I would say you three stay here, but I don't want you up here without a way to get out."

Vickie got the kids up and fed them breakfast. Maggie understood why they had to go home. Nick was very upset that they couldn't stay longer. Dan tried to explain to him that there was an emergency at work and he had to get back.

After packing up the truck, they closed up the cabin, making sure that everything was in place so the bears could not get in, climbed into the truck, and headed down the mountain to the highway to head home.

As they were heading west towards the ocean and home, Nick commented about the number of cars heading away from the beach.

"Boy, there must have been a lot of people at the beach. Look at all of the cars going home," he said.

Dan decided it was time to tell him what had happened. After the explanation of the earthquake under the water way out at sea and it causing a big gigantic wave to hit the beach and do damage to some of the buildings in the city, Nick said, "Boy, I bet I can find all kinds of sand dollars now."

Vickie turned around in her seat and said with every bit of authority that she could put into her voice, "Nicholas, you do not go anywhere near that beach, young man! Do you understand?"

Nick started to cry because his mother very rarely, if ever, spoke to him like that. "Why?" he whimpered.

Maggie took his hand and said, "Nick, right now the beach is very dangerous. I think there are a lot of very large logs on the sand, and they could move at any time. One of them could roll onto you and crush you. There could also be another big wave and pull you out to sea like it did before. There probably wouldn't be anyone there to help you this time. Please, do not go anywhere near the water. Mama and Daddy are going to be very busy for a few days, and it will be up to you and me to make sure everything is okay at home. Okay?"

"Okay, Maggie. I'm sorry I made you mad, Mama," Nick said.

"Honey, you didn't make me mad, and I am sorry I yelled at you. It just scares me to think of you getting hurt again."

Dan drove down their street with trepidation, wondering if their house was still standing. It was the house that Vickie had lived in all of her life and the house that he moved into after they were married. It was the house that they had brought both of their children to after they were born. It was their home and anchor. He prayed that it was still standing.

As he turned the corner, he saw their home standing tall and undamaged. There was a lot of debris in the front yard, and the street was partially blocked by branches from trees that had blown down, but the house looked like it was okay.

Nick got out of the car and ran around to the back of the house. "Nicholas!" Vickie yelled. He came running back hollering, "My sand dollars are still there. They did not get washed away."

"Honey, you have to stay near us for now. We don't know what we are going to find in the yard, and I don't want you to get hurt. Please don't go running off like that again," Vickie begged.

"Okay, Mom, but I had to see if my sand dollars were okay. I think Jesus was watching out for them because they remind people of him," Nicky announced.

"Okay, Nick. I'll forgive you this time, but don't do it again," she acquiesced.

"Let's get the truck unloaded, then I have to get to the lumber yard and get the equipment and men together to come into town and help with the cleanup. You need to get down to the store," Dan said to his wife.

Dan thought it was a good thing that he bought two more large blocks of ice before they headed down the highway. There was no electricity or phone service in the house. The refrigerator was off, the stove didn't work, and there were no lights.

"Nicky, would you please take your suitcase to your room and put all of your clothes away in your dresser drawers?" Vickie asked him.

"Can I watch TV, Mom?" Nick asked pleadingly.

"We don't have any electricity, Nick, so the TV is not working. Maggie is going to stay here with you. I have to go down to the store and see what I can do to help clean things up. I shouldn't be too long, but if you get hungry, there are things there to make a sandwich. I am sure Maggie will help you. And Nick, please don't leave the lid to the cooler open. We need to have that ice last for a while until we get electricity back and get the refrigerator working again."

"Okay, Mom. I wish I could watch TV, but I guess I understand. Maybe I can go over to Beth's to watch," he said, not understanding that the electricity was out all over the city.

"Honey, Beth doesn't have any electricity either, and anyway, she was still sick when we left for the cabin. I am going to stop by her house before I go down to the store to make sure she doesn't need anything," Vickie explained. Vickie knew that Ralph wasn't back from his business trip yet, and she was worried about Beth.

Fortunately, the driveway was clear, and Vickie could get her car out of the garage, but she decided to walk to the store. She wasn't sure the roads were clear. She stopped by her neighbor's house but found she was not home. She had left a note that she had gone to Eugene to her mother's house. Vickie was relieved that she had not been there by herself during the worst of the tsunami.

Dan managed to make it to the lumber yard and was very gratified that his employees were already getting the heavy trucks and the two loaders ready to move into the city.

"Boss, we assumed that you would want the trucks and loaders readied to move, so we went ahead and got them fueled up and ready to get into town. By the way, our houses are all okay. There is just a lot of debris everywhere. There are some big logs blocking Front Street, and Highway 101 is blocked, so that needs to be cleared. The highway department doesn't have the resources to do all of the work that needs to be done, so we thought that we would pitch in and do some of it. I really don't think that they will mind. Even if we can move the logs to the side of the road and clear it so traffic can get through, it will help."

"Thanks a lot, fellas. I appreciate you taking the initiative on this. Let's get going. I will lead the way with my truck, and you follow. We probably need to get 101 cleared through town as soon as we can, then work on Front Street. I haven't seen it yet. Is it pretty bad?" Dan asked his foreman as he was climbing into the cab of his truck.

"Yeah, it's bad!" the foreman answered.

# CHAPTER 7

---

The IGA grocery store was a mess. The building itself was relatively undamaged. It was a concrete block building and held up to the force of the water, but all of the windows were broken out, and everything inside was all over the floor. Bottles were broken, and the contents were spilled all over the place. There was soda pop, cleaning liquid, syrup, pickles, and everything that was packaged in glass bottles or jars all mixed together on the floor. The worst part was all of the glass. There were shards of glass embedded in everything.

George Barnes, the store manager, had pulled some heavy leather gloves off of the shelf and handed them to everyone who was working on the cleanup. "Vickie, I am sure glad to see you. We need your help. Here, take these gloves and put them on, and be very careful where you walk. I am glad to see you in heavy shoes. There is glass everywhere. I found some boxes of large heavy-duty trash bags. I am asking people to start picking up the perishable food first and putting it in the bags and taking them out to the parking lot. The two garbage trucks are making constant runs from here and other stores to one of the fields a mile out of town and dumping the bags. The mayor has people patrolling the area so that there won't be any looters. So far, I have not opened the cash registers to get the money out," George said quietly to Vickie. "No one has been in here who doesn't belong. Would you please see if you can get the registers open and put all of the cash into this bag? With this new system, I never did learn to open them when the power went out."

George called them cash registers, but they were really only cash drawers. Some of them were turned on their sides, but Vickie managed to get all of them opened. She was able to remove all of the cash, checks, and other information that was needed to balance each register, including the information on the credit card transactions. She did it quietly, and she hoped without anyone realizing what she was doing. The safe in George's office was still intact, and she was able to put the bag into the safe, close it, and lock it. George looked at her with an immense look of gratitude for taking care of that. The day of the tsunami was a busy one at the store. People were stocking up on supplies in case they needed them, and a lot of people were buying food to eat on the road while they were leaving town.

When she finished with the cash drawers, she got busy and started working in the produce department. She had tears in her eyes as she was tossing all of the fresh produce into garbage bags to be thrown out. Much of it had little pieces of glass embedded in it. They had to dispose of thousands and thousands of dollars' worth of food. IGA was a large grocery chain and would absorb the loss and would, she assumed, rebuild, but it would take time. In the meantime, the town would be without a grocery store.

After Maggie and Nick had their sandwiches, they got to work and started cleaning up some of the debris in their yard. Maggie brought out large black trash bags, and they quickly filled up several bags from their yard.

"Maggie, I think we should clean up Beth and Ralph's yard too. It is a mess, and it would be nice to help them," Nick suggested.

"You are really a good kid, Nick. That's a great idea." Although she was going to suggest it, she gave the credit to Nick. He always felt so important when he thought of an idea that she or their parents liked.

"Are all of your sand dollars okay, Nick?" Maggie asked, knowing that he was relieved that they were all okay. He loved talking about all of the shells that they had found and how much money he thought he would make from selling them.

"I think we will have to wait a little while now. The stores that would have bought them from you were all on Front Street, and Dad said that he heard that most of the buildings were knocked down. They will have to rebuild them before they can buy any sand dollars. But we can sure save them, and maybe when we can walk on the beach again, we can find some more. There should be lots of them down there," Maggie told him.

"I wish I could go down there now," Nick said yearningly.

"I know, but you just can't. It is much too dangerous. Like Mom said, there are logs down there that could shift and roll over on you. They are big logs like the ones at Dad's lumber yard. You know the rules there. Well, they are the same on the beach now. And we don't want to take a chance of another big wave coming in and pulling you out into the water. We might not be able to get you back," Maggie explained.

"I know all that, but I still wish I could go down there. I could probably find thousands of sand dollars," Nick announced.

Maggie was worried now. She was afraid that Nick would go off on his own and head for the beach. She would have to tell her mom and dad about this talk so that all three of them could keep a very close watch on his activities. They were going to have to figure out something to do to keep him busy and his mind off the beach.

Maggie was also concerned about her friends. She had not heard from Jeannie, and with no phone service, she couldn't call her. Maybe tomorrow or the next day, she and Nick could walk over to Jeannie's house to see her. Maggie hoped that she was okay. School was supposed to start in another month. It would be the beginning of her sophomore year. No more of being the lowest grade in the school.

Both Dan and Vickie came home that evening, tired, dirty, and hungry. There wasn't much that Maggie knew how to fix, but she could make a pretty good sandwich. She had sandwiches and a salad ready for them. They ate off of paper plates since they did not have any hot water to wash the dishes with.

"Thank goodness the fireplace wasn't damaged. I'll build a fire so that we can at least have a little heat and some light from the flames. Mom brought some candles home that she found at the store, so we can use them as light in the bedrooms. They will be lit only for a little while, though. We do not want to cause a fire by falling asleep with a candle burning," Dan told his children.

"Dad, Maggie and I cleaned up part of Beth and Ralph's yard too. Did you see it?" Nick asked, very proud of himself. "It was my idea too."

Vickie walked into the room at that moment, looked at her family, and started to cry. "What's wrong, Mama?" Nick asked, concerned for his mother. "Are you hurt?"

"No, honey. I am just very proud of you and very happy that we still have our home and we are not hurt. I love you all so much, and I thank God that we are all together. There are a lot of families in town who have lost their homes and businesses and do not know where their families are right now. Let's remember those people when we say our prayers tonight," Vickie said to her family as she hugged all of them.

Every resource available to the towns along the Central Oregon Coast was brought to bear in the cleanup. Not only the local police, but the State Patrol were on duty guarding properties, and the Governor called out the National Guard to patrol and guard against looting. The Florence Lumber Mill supplied plywood so that people could board up their businesses along Front Street. As soon as the street was cleared so that the shop owners could get access to their stores, they were allowed in to try and salvage what they could. Almost all of the stores had glass windows, so glass shards were everywhere, and the clinic was overloaded with people with cut feet and hands. There was a call out for medical personnel to come into the area and help. The National Guard provided portable tents for medical clinics, and the Red Cross became a strong presence in Florence and all up and down the central coast.

Because the newspaper office was about eight blocks back from the beachfront, it was not damaged. Normally, the paper published weekly, but during this crisis, the owner and publisher of the Siuslaw News, Simon Alden, was publishing a one-sheet newspaper daily and distributing it for free to several areas around the city. He had lists of areas where people could get help and daily updates on roads opened and progress being made on the cleanup. He also posted notices for people looking for loved ones. The tsunami had resulted in some deaths in the community, and there were still some people not accounted for.

There was a big push to get the power back on and to get the phone lines working again. The clinic, newspaper office, and county and city buildings had emergency generators, but people needed their homes to have power so that they could preserve their food properly.

Dan was gone from morning to night removing logs from roads and buildings. His loader was in constant use lifting heavy walls that had come down on Front Street. The priority during the initial aftermath of the tsunami was search and rescue. Everyone but two families was accounted for. Most of the people had moved to higher ground, either to the mountains like the Roberts or closer to Eugene, far out of the line of the waves. Two deaths were reported, and those were not storm-related. Both of the deaths were older people in the assisted living center who were ill to begin with. Both were from heart attacks. It was sad to lose them, but at least there were no deaths from the tsunami.

Finally, both of the missing families were found. They had gone to Portland together before any notification was made about a possible tsunami. Because phones were down for a couple of days, they were unable to let anyone know where they were.

Dan's loaders were too heavy to be moved onto the sand to try and either remove or reposition the logs. He was afraid that they would get stuck in the sand, and then nothing could remove them. He was able to get one of them positioned just beyond the sea wall so that it could reach some of the closest logs. His crew was able to remove about 10 large logs from the beach that were in danger of rolling off of each other and causing serious injury or death to anyone in the way.

Vickie spent about four days working at the grocery store trying to clean up. No walls had collapsed at the store, but there were no windows left, and everything was exposed to the weather. Fortunately, the weather had stayed fair during all of the cleanup, but it was unpredictable on the Oregon Coast. A storm could come up at any time, and rain could come pouring down. There was a sense of urgency about getting the cleanup done. After four days of intensive cleanup work, George Barnes told his employees that they would not be needed anymore. The company could not afford to continue to pay their salaries with no money coming in.

In a meeting with his employees, he said, "I am waiting to hear from corporate headquarters when they will start to repair the building and restock. You know that you all have your jobs waiting for you when we do open again, but until then, I cannot pay you. You will, of course, be paid for your time helping with the cleanup. As soon as electricity is restored and we can get refrigeration up and running again, we will hopefully be able to stock a few necessities, but until then, there will be signs on the building directing customers."

Vickie was looking forward to having some time at home without worrying about having to go to work. She needed to spend some time with her kids. Both of them were growing up and changing fast, and she was missing out on a lot of it. She knew that this would be coming. She and Dan had talked about her staying at home. Dan knew that Vickie was eager to be at home with the kids. Maggie really needed her guidance as she was proceeding through her teenage years, and Noah always needed someone around, but he needed to be able to expand his horizons too. Vickie could help him do that safely. After his accident at the beach, they were both terrified that he would get hurt again.

Both Dan and Vickie decided that they would go to their investment broker in Lincoln City and arrange to supplement their income with a monthly amount from their savings. It was obvious that Nick would not be going on to college, and they had a good investment program set up for his continued care, so the amount that they had allocated for his education could be used to supplement Dan's income from the business. Also, he might be able to repair or update some of his equipment.

Vickie was thrilled with their new plan and wanted to tell the kids at dinnertime that night. She hoped that they would be glad that she was going to be home. First of all, Maggie would be off of her mandatory

"Saturdays with Nick" duty, and Vickie knew that she would be very glad about that. She hadn't had much of a social life this summer. School would be starting soon, and she wanted to have a little time with both of them before they went off to school again. It was hard to believe that Maggie would be a sophomore in high school. Nick would go back to the special education class at the elementary school, but this year they would try to integrate him into the regular fourth-grade class. Vickie was hoping that he would do well and that the other kids in the class would adjust to him. Time would tell, but at least she would be available if he needed her.

# CHAPTER 8

Neither Dan nor Vickie had paid much attention to the monthly statements that came from their investment counselor. They had set aside Vickie's inheritance for their children and had not used any of it. When her mother died, she lived off of an annuity that was set up for her when she was small. Her mother's house had no mortgage, her car was paid off, and all she had to worry about were the monthly bills and the taxes on her property. When she and Dan married, they made the decision to live off of his income. After Nick was born, Vickie went to work part-time at the grocery store to supplement their income. It was obvious that Nick would need additional care, but their income was not large enough to provide the specialized care that he was going to need as he grew older. About that time, George Barnes, the manager of the IGA Grocery, offered Vickie a full-time job as a cashier.

Beth Freeman, Vickie and Dan's neighbor, offered to take care of Nick while Vickie was working, and Nick loved to play with her son, so Vickie went to work on a full-time basis. The added income helped them maintain a comfortable lifestyle and have a few of the extras that they wanted. They made a conscious decision when they were married to not spend that money until their children needed it for college. Neither of them paid any attention to the statements that came in monthly. They didn't understand them, so they put them in a file for tax purposes and around the first of February every year, gave their CPA the file to prepare their taxes.

They didn't know how much money they had until they walked into Isaac Steinberg's office on a Monday morning the second week of September. The kids had started back to school, and Dan had taken the morning off to make all the arrangements so that Vickie would not have to work.

Isaac and Annie Steinberg owned and operated Steinberg Investments. Their office was several blocks from the beach and was not damaged by the tsunami, but the majority of their clients had either catastrophic or major damage to their properties. Isaac's family immigrated to the United States in 1937 from Nazi-occupied Germany. His father, mother, two brothers, and two sisters were all able to get visas to come. They were among the last of the German Jews to be able to leave Germany and travel to safety. All of the rest of Simon's family were lost to the death camps. Isaac was the baby of the family and only two years old when they arrived in America. He had no firsthand knowledge of their boat ride across the Atlantic but loved to tell stories that he had heard from his parents and siblings.

Isaac met Annie in New York City, married her, and together they decided to come to the West Coast to live. Isaac was as round as he was tall. He did not remember much about Germany, but he knew that he loved German pastries, and his Annie was one of the best bakers in Florence.

Annie greeted Dan and Vickie with open arms when they walked into the office that Monday morning. She had a habit of greeting everyone she knew with open arms, so both the Roberts were prepared for a huge hug before they were ushered into Isaac's office.

After some talk about the tsunami and the damage to their city, Dan got down to the business of why they were there.

"Isaac, the grocery is going to be closed for a while, and George cannot afford to pay his employees with no money coming in, so Vickie's going to be without a job. It will be nice to have her home, and the kids are excited about having her around more, but we are going to be strapped for money without her income. We are here to see about possibly getting a monthly income from her investments to compensate for the loss of her income," Dan explained.

Isaac looked at both of them carefully. "Do either of you know what your investments are worth?" Isaac countered.

Vickie answered by saying, "Not really. We don't pay much attention to the statements you send us. I just put them in a file and hand the file to you at tax time. Don't we have enough for a small monthly amount?"

Isaac just stared at them and then started to laugh. He took a yellow highlighter and ran it through a number at the bottom of a line of numbers and turned it around to show it to Dan and Vickie. They both looked at the number and then at each other and then back at the number.

Vickie whispered, "That can't be true. Mama didn't leave me that much when she died. You have made a mistake someplace."

"No mistake, Vickie! This is the total amount you inherited when she died 22 years ago. It was invested wisely for you, and this is the amount it has grown to now. I have notified you every time I proposed moving some of the money around, and you have always told me to do what I thought was best. I guess what I thought was best was the best because this is the amount your investments are worth now," Isaac explained.

"You can double the amount you are asking for if you want to. As you can see by these figures, you are very well off and will not have to worry about your future if you are careful," Isaac explained to the startled couple.

"We had no idea it was this much. I knew that the fund had grown since Mom died, but I had no idea how much," Vickie said with wonder. "Holy cow, Dan, you could even buy a new truck like you have been saying you need," she added.

"Let's just concentrate on this for now," Dan said as he looked at Vickie. "I can't think of anything else right now." Dan wrote a figure down on a piece of paper and handed it to Vickie to look at. She nodded her agreement, and Dan said, "Isaac, can you arrange to have this amount transferred to our checking account on the first of each month? That would make it easier than for us to have to deposit a check every month."

"Sure, I can. It will be done beginning the first of October. Will that be okay, or do you need an additional amount for the balance of September?" Dan asked.

"No, George was able to pay all of the employees for September," Vickie assured him.

Dan and Vickie walked out of Isaac's office still stunned by what he had shown them. They got into Dan's truck and drove home in silence, each thinking their own thoughts.

Vickie made lunch for Dan before he had to go to the lumber yard. He had some work that he had to get done today. He had very good office help, but there were some things he had to take care of himself.

"Honey, while I was sitting in Isaac's office trying to absorb what he had shown us, I was thinking of the cabin. It would not cost very much money to put a refrigerator in there. We have electricity. All we would have to do is run another line in, and we could buy a used refrigerator for very little money. It would save us having to go down the hill for ice every two days. What do you think?" Dan asked.

"I think it's a great idea. Just don't try and get rid of the wood stove. I love that stove, and nothing tastes better than our meals cooked on it," she begged.

"Okay! No electric stove. Just the refrigerator. Maybe someday we can upgrade to running water, maybe even put a water heater in so we can have hot water. But that's in the future. Let's concentrate on a refrigerator for now," Dan said.

They both laughed at themselves. They felt like kids in a candy shop at that moment.

"Dan, I do not want to say anything to Maggie about this. Sure, we can tell her that we are getting a refrigerator for the cabin, but I do not think it is a good idea to say anything about how much money we have. It doesn't need to be broadcast all over town," Vickie explained to her husband.

"I agree. She doesn't need to know. She's too young to understand the implications of other people knowing our business," Dan commented.

After Dan went to work, Vickie cleaned up the kitchen and then went to pick Nicky up from school. He didn't like walking home. He said the other kids teased him because he was not smart enough and couldn't be in a regular classroom. Vickie was heartsick for her son. He didn't deserve that, but there was not much she could do about it.

When she drove up to the school, she found Maggie standing next to Nicky. "What are you doing here, honey?" she asked her daughter.

"I decided that I would walk home with Nick. We have some things to talk about regarding our sand dollar project," she stated matter-of-factly.

"Yeah, Mom! We are going to start a business. Just Maggie and me," Nick announced proudly. "But, Mom, we need some supplies.

Maggie says we need to go to a craft store. What is a craft store, Mom?"

Vickie laughed at her son. "A craft store is where you buy all the supplies that you need to do any kind of craft. A craft is either painting, working with wood, knitting like Beth does, or sewing like I do. I would have to check to see where the nearest craft store is now. There was one in Newport, but I don't know if the tsunami damaged it or not. I will check and see, and maybe next Saturday we can go to one. What kind of supplies do you need?"

"We need paint, brushes, and some kind of sealer. I have been doing some research on painting on shells. We would need to use acrylic paint and have several different kinds of brushes. We could use spray-on sealer after the paint dries," Maggie explained.

"We might have to go into Eugene to find what you want, but maybe Dad would go with us, and we could make a day of it on Saturday," Vickie added.

Maggie had decided that she enjoyed walking to school with Nicky in the mornings. The high school was right next door to the elementary school, so she did not have to go out of her way, and Nicky was so excited to be walking with his big sister. No one bothered him when she was around. Vickie was relishing the fact that she did not have to get up and get dressed for work early in the morning. She could have a second cup of coffee and relax before her day began. There was one day that Dan had no pressing problems at the lumber yard and stayed home for another hour with her. They loved that extra time together.

They decided to go into Eugene on Saturday, go to Michael's, the craft store, and get what the kids needed for their sand dollar project, and maybe look for a refrigerator for the cabin. Dan was anxious to get one installed. He had talked to a couple of electricians that he knew and was sure that he could run the line into the house himself.

While they were in Eugene, he would be able to pick up all of the supplies he needed. It had been a long time since they had made any changes to the cabin. The last major change was adding the second bedroom when they found out they were going to have another baby.

Vickie and Maggie would also make a trip to the fabric store. Maggie spent most of her time in jeans and either t-shirts or sweatshirts, but she would want a new dress for the sophomore dance. It would be her first formal dance of her high school years, and Vickie knew she would want something special. The clothes that Vickie made for her daughter were just a little different and unique. They didn't look like anything found on the racks at the clothing stores. Not many of her friends knew that her mother made all of her clothes for her. Maggie was very proud to wear "homemade" clothes.

"Come on, Nick, get into the car. It's time to go!" Dan hollered at his son.

"I forgot my list, Dad," Nick said as he scrambled into the back seat of the car.

"How come we're not going in your truck, Dad? I like riding up high in your truck," Nick asked.

"We are going clear into Eugene today, and the truck takes a lot more gasoline to get there and back home. The car is a lot more comfortable anyway," Dan answered with a grin on his face and a glance at his wife.

The highway from Florence to Eugene was a very good road, but heavily forested in places, and it took a lot of concentration to drive. Most of the time, Dan had both hands on the steering wheel, but on straight, open stretches of highway, he would take Vickie's hand. After being married for 16 years, he was still in awe of her and loved her even more than he thought he ever could.

Eugene was bustling on that Saturday morning in September. The University of Oregon's first semester had just started, and the town was ablaze with green and gold. The Oregon Ducks football team was on top of the rankings again, and everyone was talking about the Rose Bowl and were sure the Ducks would make it this year.

"I think it would be a good idea if we all stuck together today. I know that sometimes when we come to Eugene, we split up and Maggie and I do our thing, and you and Nick go and do yours, but it is so crowded here today that I would feel much better if we stuck together," Vickie announced to Dan and the kids.

"I agree!" said Dan. "The crowds are thick today. Parking was ridiculous."

# CHAPTER 9

an and Vickie waited by the cash register while Maggie and Nicky searched the painting section for just what they wanted to paint their sand dollars. Maggie had done some research and found out what kind of paint and brushes they would need. Vickie had given them an initial budget of $50.00 for all of the supplies that they would need to get started. She was sure that Nicky would want to buy one of everything, but also knew that Maggie had a pretty good head for money and would keep him on budget.

"Maggie, look at all these colors," Nicky exclaimed. "There are so many to choose from."

"Nick, remember how we talked about only using colors that matched the beach, sea, and sky? We need to stick with those colors to begin with. We have to prove to Mom and Dad that we can do this before they let us spend any more money on more paint. And remember that we have to get the acrylic paint. I wrote the word down for you so you can find it on the jars," Maggie explained.

Nick had ahold of the piece of paper that Maggie gave him and was looking carefully at all of the bottles and tubes to find just the right word.

"Here it is, Maggie!" Nick said excitedly. "I found it!"

"Okay. Let's pick out the colors that are like the sand, sky, and sea. What colors would those be?" Maggie asked Nick.

"The sky and the ocean are blue and sometimes green. The moon is white and the sun is yellow. The sand can be grey or tan. Maybe we should get all of those colors," Nick said as he looked hopefully up at his sister.

"I think that is a great idea, Nick," she answered. They put one of each of the colors in their basket and went on to the brushes. "We need a sponge brush and two bristle brushes. Remember, the sand dollars aren't really large, so we don't need a really large brush," Maggie explained.

"Are these okay, Maggie?" Nicky asked.

"Perfect!" she answered.

They walked up to the cash register where their parents were waiting to pay for the supplies. Nick was excited to show them what they had picked out.

"Let's pay for it first, Sport," his dad said. "Then when we get to the car, we can look at what you bought."

"Can we go home now so Maggie and I can start painting?" he asked his dad.

"We have some more errands to do while we are here, and don't you want some lunch first?" Vickie asked.

"I guess so," said a deflated Nicky. He perked up a bit and asked if they could go to McDonald's. Maggie groaned at the thought. "Nick, there are so many nice restaurants in Eugene. You go to McDonald's all the time at home."

"But I like McDonald's," Nicky moaned.

"Sorry, Sport! You are outnumbered this time. Mom, Maggie, and I want pizza for lunch," Dan announced.

"Well, Dad, that's my second choice," Nick announced.

"Good! Pizza it is," Dan replied.

After a family-sized pizza and a lot of root beer were consumed, they were off to the electrical supply store so that Dan could get what he needed to add another line into the cabin for a refrigerator, then they were on their way home.

Both Maggie and Nicky were dozing in the back seat on the way home. Dan had the radio on softly, listening to a soft rock music station. All of a sudden, a bulletin came on telling people to stay off of the beach. There were higher than normal waves expected to hit the central Oregon beaches. The authorities were worried that the high tides would dislodge some of the logs that had not been removed from the coastline after the tsunami. It was still dangerous to walk on the beach. It had been two months since the tsunami hit the beach in Florence, and the stores along Front Street were still in shambles. The owners were trying to clean up the mess of mud and sand that had poured into the buildings, but Front Street was still a jumble of splintered wood and broken glass. There was no way to secure their buildings because there wasn't much of their buildings left to secure.

Dan glanced at Vickie and said, "We better speed up and get home. No telling if they are going to need my equipment again. I better be there if they need me." Vickie just nodded as Dan drove home as fast as he safely could.

The waves were very high coming onto the shore, and they did dislodge some of the logs that could not be moved earlier, but they did not go over the sea wall. Dan and some of his crew took his loader and a log truck and were able to get the loader onto Front Street and reach over the sea wall to pick up some of the dislodged logs and load them onto the truck. The logs were still waterlogged and would have to sit at the mill for some time before they could be cut, but the town council and the mayor were very glad to get them off of the beach. There were still quite a few logs left, but they would pose little hazard to anyone on the beach. The mayor decided to open the beach up for use again. Even though there were no shops on Front Street and no grocery store, people were still coming to the beach for holidays, and the locals wanted to get onto the sand again.

Nicky was clamoring to get to the beach to find more sand dollars to dry out and paint. He was upset because Vickie would not let him miss school to look for them.

"But Mom, it is going to be our business. We need to find as many as possible," he begged.

"But Nicky, you have to go to school. How do you think you can run a business if you don't have an education?" Vickie answered back to her son, with a grin on her face. "If you and Maggie finish your homework, you can go down there for a while this evening."

"But Mom, you find the best sand dollars in the early morning," he continued to beg.

"No more, Nicholas! You will go to school. If the best time to find sand dollars is the early morning, you can go on Saturday. But you are not to go by yourself. Do you understand, Nick?" she said with authority.

"Yes, Mom! I don't want to have another accident like I had before," Nick answered.

"Now go and get your sweater and back pack. Maggie is ready to walk with you to school."

After Nicky turned off to go to his school, Maggie met up with some of her friends. Her best friend Jeannie said, "Haven't seen much of you lately Mags. You sure have been spending a lot of time with your pip-squeak of a brother."

"Do not talk about my brother like that Jeannie. He is really a great kid and I like spending time with him," Maggie said with authority. "I am helping him with a project and having a lot of fun doing it."

"OK!" Jeannie said with a louder than usual . "What kind of project?"

"Actually, Nick has asked me not to tell anyone right now. He wants to get farther along with it before he lets people know what we are doing," Maggie announced.

"Well, we never spend any time together anymore. I miss you, Mags," Jeannie complained.

"You know I had to take care of Nick on Saturdays during the summer, and during the cleanup, I was busy all of the time. He and I cleaned up both our own yard and several of our neighbors' yards. My mom and dad were super busy during the cleanup, so I had to be home with Nick. He badly wanted to go to the beach, but he couldn't, and I had to be there to make sure he didn't. We almost lost him last summer, and I didn't want anything like that to ever happen again. Anyway, like I said, I enjoy spending time with him. He is very sweet and funny," Maggie explained.

The next Monday was a parent-teacher conference day for both the elementary and high schools, and the kids didn't have to go to school. Vickie suggested that it would be a good day for Maggie to take Nick to the beach to look for more sand dollars and maybe afterwards start painting on the ones they had ready.

"Can we, Maggie? Can we please go on Saturday?" Nick begged his sister.

"Sure, but we have to go early," Maggie said. "That means just when it gets light enough to see."

Nicky was up before it was light, dressed, and eating a bowl of cereal at the kitchen table when Maggie came into the kitchen. "Are you ready, Maggie?" Nicky asked.

"Let me get some breakfast. It is still too dark outside to see the sand dollars, and we have to be able to see if there is any danger on the beach," Maggie explained to a very excited Nicky.

Maggie was sad every time she walked along Front Street and saw the ruins of the stores still there. Only a few of the businesses had started rebuilding their properties. A lot of them would not return. They had lost everything and couldn't afford to rebuild and restock their shops. The grocery store was about a week away from reopening. They were restocking now. All of the windows had been replaced with double-pane glass, and the checkout lines and registers were better secured to the floor. A new, more powerful generator was installed. George Barnes wanted Vickie to come back to work, but she and Dan had decided that it was time for her to stay home and enjoy being a homemaker and taking care of her daughter and son.

Maggie was thinking about all of this when she and Nicky were walking to the beach, and she realized that Nick was not right beside her. She could see him already down on the sand, looking for shells.

"Nicholas!" she yelled. When anyone said Nicholas to him, he knew he was in trouble. He stopped and looked up at his sister, who was just walking down the steps to the sand. "Never run ahead like that unless I tell you that it's okay. We have to watch for any dangers on the sand. Some of these logs could still come loose and roll onto you."

"Sorry, Maggie," Nick said very meekly. "I was just so excited to find more sand dollars."

"I know, Nick, but you have to be careful too."

Nick and Maggie found eight good sand dollars that morning. They found a lot of them that were broken, and Nick felt sad for each broken one they found, but he was excited when he found a good one.

Dan had put a cover over their patio two years ago, and Vickie set up an area under the cover for the kids to do their painting. She also cleaned off the window sills in the kitchen and dining nook, covered the sills with oilcloth, and prepared a drying area for the sand dollars. Vickie was becoming enthusiastic about the kids' project also.

The first sand dollars that Nicky painted were a little messy and not really good, but he improved rapidly, and both Dan and Vickie were amazed at his ability to put colors together. He painted some beautiful sand dollars, and both his parents thought that he could sell them.

"Why don't you talk to George and see if he would set up a table in the store? Since the gift shops are not open yet, maybe people going into the grocery store would notice them and want to buy one as a souvenir," Dan asked. "I really think that people will buy them. He is really good!"

Vickie went in to see George about setting up an area for the kids to sell their sand dollars. She took three of them in with her to show George what Nick was doing and how good they were. "Did you say Nick or Maggie painted these?" George asked.

"Nick painted these. Maggie has done a few, but she is leaving most of the painting up to Nick," Vickie explained.

"Bring him in, and we will negotiate a price. I will buy them from him and sell them myself. They are good, Vickie. He has talent," George told a very proud mother.

Dan was home early that evening. He loved having Vickie there when he got home. He was not a very good cook, and when she had to work late, he had to get supper ready for the kids. They complained bitterly about their dad's cooking. He could warm over leftovers okay, but that was about it. With his wife at home, he came home to happy kids and a meal about ready to put on the table. The tradeoff was that he and the kids cleaned up after supper. He would load the dishwasher, and Nick and Maggie would wash and dry the pots and pans.

At supper, Vickie told Dan and the kids what George had said about the sand dollars.

"Nick, I took some of your painted sand dollars in to the store to show him and asked him if you could set up a table and sell them. George wants to buy them from you and sell them himself. He thinks you have a real talent for painting. He likes the way you put your colors together. What do you think?" Vickie announced to Nick and Maggie.

Nick looked at Maggie. She was grinning. "I told you they were pretty, and I thought they would sell," she said to Nick. She looked at her mom and said, "I wasn't sure if we could sell them around here. All of the gift shops on Front Street that would have bought them are closed down. Mr. Barnes really likes them?" she asked.

"He does. He thinks they will sell easily, especially because they are done by a local artist," Vickie said as she grinned at Nick.

"Great job, kids! With your business going, maybe I can retire and stay home with Mom, and you can support us for a change," Dan said as he also grinned at his children.

"Oh, Dad! Maggie and I will be making some money, but I don't think it will be enough at first to support us," Nick said with an equally large grin on his face.

"That's okay, Sport. I will continue to support you and your sister. That's my job, and I love it!"

# CHAPTER 10

———————◆◆◆————◆◆◆————

Nicky and Maggie finished ten sand dollars. Nicky painted them, and Maggie sprayed the sealer on them. Their mother felt that she was a little better able to handle the spray can and get a good seal on the shells.

After they were good and dry, Vickie and Maggie carefully packed them into a box, and they all walked down to the grocery store to talk to George Barnes.

"Hello, Mr. Barnes," Nicky said, putting his hand out to shake the older man's hand. "My mother said that you were interested in purchasing some of my painted sand dollars," Nicky announced in a very business-like manner. "I am here to sell you some if the price is right."

George Barnes grinned at Vickie and said, "I am indeed interested in purchasing some of your beautiful sand dollars. What were you thinking of asking for them, Nicholas?"

"Well, they do take a lot of work. First, I have to find the good ones on the beach, then they have to be cleaned and dried before I can paint them. Maggie puts the sealer on them. I am not very good with spray cans. I was thinking maybe 50 cents each," Nicky said.

"Oh my, but I think they are worth a lot more than that, Nicholas. I was prepared to offer you $1.50 each for them. I think I can sell them for $3.00 each, which would double my investment," Mr. Barnes announced.

Nicky's eyes widened at the offer of $1.50 each. He wasn't very good at arithmetic yet, but he knew that it was a lot of money. He looked at his mother and Maggie for guidance. They both gave him a nod, and he said to George Barnes, "Mr. Barnes, it's a deal!"

George Barnes laughed and asked Nicky if he wanted a check or cash. Nick looked at his mom, and she said, "Let's do a check, Nicky. We can take it to the bank, and you and Maggie can open your own business account."

"Thank you, Mr. Barnes. I can have more ready for you in a few days. My mom says I have to go to school, so I can spend all of my time painting, but I will do them when my homework is finished," Nicky explained.

"Nicholas, it is very important that you get a good education. You have quite a talent at painting sand dollars, but you need to know how to read and write and do your numbers to be able to run a good business. You keep doing your schoolwork. I will accept your sand dollars anytime you have some ready for sale."

George Barnes wrote a check to Nicholas Roberts for $19.50. The amount included the three that Vickie had taken in to show him earlier.

Maggie had told her mom and dad that she wanted Nick to have all of the profits from the sale of his sand dollars. It was his idea and mostly his work, and she was just helping him. So when Vickie took them to the bank to open a savings account, it was opened in the name of Nicholas Roberts, with Vickie as the responsible party since Nicholas was a minor. The bank manager, Peter Swenson, handed Nicky his savings account record book showing a balance of $19.50.

"Good luck, Nicholas! I will go over to the grocery store and take a look at your sand dollars. I might buy one for my wife. She likes things like that," Mr. Swenson told him.

Dan was home from work when his family walked in the door. "You are home early. Is everything okay?" Vickie asked him.

Before he could answer his wife, Nicholas had run up to him shouting, "Look, Dad. I have a bank book. Mr. Barnes paid me $1.50 for my sand dollars. He wrote me a check, and we took it to the bank to open a savings account. Maggie didn't want any of the money, so the account is in my name. Mom had to be on there too because I am too young, but Mr. Swenson said that was just a formal—oh, something like that!"

"A formality?" Dan asked with a grin.

"Yeah—a formality," Nick answered.

"You be sure to put that in a safe place, Nick," Vickie told him. "Remember, Mr. Swenson said that you need to bring it to the bank anytime you make a deposit so he can record it. That way you can keep track of how much money you have."

"Okay, Mom. I am going to check to see if the other sand dollars are ready to be painted," Nick said as he ran off to the back patio.

Maggie had gone to her room, and Vickie said to her husband, "What's wrong, Dan? Why are you home so early?"

"I didn't want to say anything in front of the kids, but I need you to take me in to see Doc Jansen. Ask Maggie to keep an eye on Nick while we run an errand. Tell her it has to do with the lumber yard or something, but don't tell her where we are going," Dan asked Vickie in a weak voice.

"Dan, you are scaring me!" Vickie said fearfully.

"Honey, just do as I ask, please," he said.

Vickie did as Dan asked and found him getting into the passenger side of her car. She ran around to drive him to the doctor. As she was driving, Dan slumped over onto her shoulder, gave a groan, and passed out.

"Dan, Dan! Wake up! What is wrong, sweetheart? I will have you at the doctor in a minute. Wake up, Dan!" Vickie was crying and yelling at Dan.

She pulled up in front of the clinic, got out, and ran to the door, yelling for Doc Jansen to come.

The doctor and his nurse, along with Vickie, got Dan into the clinic and into an examining room. The nurse made Vickie stay outside while the doctor checked Dan's pulse and breathing.

Vickie was sitting in the waiting room, beside herself with worry and fear. It had been 45 minutes since she had driven Dan to the clinic, and the doctor had not been out to talk to her at all. The receptionist had to almost physically hold her back from going into the room to see her husband.

After a few more minutes, the doctor buzzed the receptionist from his office and asked her to show Vickie in.

As Vickie walked into the office, she had a feeling that she was never going to see her husband alive again. She knew he was dead!

"Vickie, I am so sorry, but Dan didn't make it. He had a severe heart attack. I really don't know how he ever drove home from the lumber yard. It was sheer will, I guess."

Vickie sat there stunned. She didn't cry or scream or say anything. She was just stunned. After a few minutes, she said to the doctor, "I have to get home and tell the kids. Maggie is watching Nicholas. I don't know how to tell them that their dad will never be coming home again."

With those words, Vickie started to sob. Doctor Jansen called for his nurse to come in to stay with her for a few minutes while he talked to his receptionist. He had no pressing appointments for the rest of the day and asked his receptionist to reschedule all of them. He was going to drive Mrs. Roberts home and be with her when she told her kids that their dad had died. The Roberts family went to the same church as he did, and he called Reverend Silas to join him at the Roberts house.

Almost the entire town showed up for the funeral of Daniel Roberts. The Florence United Methodist Church was overflowing. The ladies of the church had arranged a lunch buffet to be held in the social hall after the service. Dan had requested that he be cremated and his ashes be scattered into the woods near their cabin.

Vickie, Maggie, and Nick were all in a state of shock. Maggie understood what had happened to her dad, but Nicky wasn't sure he understood what death was. He knew that the sand dollars he picked up off of the beach were dead, but he didn't understand how or why a person died, especially his own dad.

People were in and out of his house all day, some of them crying. Mama and Maggie were crying too. He didn't know if he should be crying too. Mr. Barnes came into the living room where Nick was sitting and sat down beside him. He asked Nick how the painting was coming along. He let him know that he was ready for some more sand dollars to sell.

"Did you sell the ones you had, Mr. Barnes?" Nick asked, looking up at him with a hopeful look in his eyes.

"I have one left, Nicholas. My customers really like them," George explained to Nick.

"I have some more I can give to you now," Nick announced.

"Why don't you wait until Monday, Nicholas? Then I will be able to write you a check for them," George said.

"Okay, Mr. Barnes," Nick answered. "I will bring them to the store on Monday, but it will have to be after school. Mom and Dad say I have to go to school every day."

George Barnes felt very sad for Nicholas and for Vickie and Maggie also. It was going to be especially hard for Nicholas to get used to not having his dad around.

Finally, the house was empty of all the visitors, and Vickie and Maggie sprawled on the sofa. Beth and a couple of the other neighbor ladies had cleaned up the kitchen, labeled all of the dishes that people brought over, and put all that they could into the refrigerator, said goodbye to Vickie, and left by the back door. Nick was out on the back deck counting the sand dollars that he still had to paint. Neither Beth nor Maggie thought that he was aware yet that his dad would not be coming home again. Throughout this past week of shock, confusion, and planning for a funeral, Nicky had been detached from the proceedings. Several times he said that he hoped his dad would be home for the party, or when his dad came home, he wanted to show him his latest painted sand dollars.

Vickie was overwhelmed with the responsibility of raising her children by herself, especially one with special needs. She had read many books on raising children with mental and physical problems, but she hadn't found one yet that told her how to do it without the man she loved beside her. She was also concerned about Maggie losing her teenage years and growing up too fast. At least Vickie was eighteen when her parents were killed and was considered an adult. And she had met Dan. Now she was without him.

Besides her kids, Vickie had to make decisions on what to do with the lumber yard and the cabin in the woods. She did not want to get rid of the cabin. It was a retreat from the busy life, and it was a place very dear to hers and Dan's hearts.

As far as the lumber yard and business were concerned, she would probably sell it if she could get a decent price for it. She would check with Walter Kane, the owner of the Florence Lumber Mill. He might know of someone who would be interested in buying the mill with all of the equipment included. The only thing that Vickie wanted was Dan's pickup truck.

Because of the lumber yard, the investments that they had, and the minor children, Vickie knew that she needed an attorney who specialized in estate planning to advise her on how to proceed with a guarantee that the kids were taken care of if anything should happen to her. With no parents or siblings for either her or Dan, she had to find someone who would take care of them. She didn't have any close girlfriends growing up. She was always a loner, especially after her parents died. She took care of herself. She supposed that Beth Freeman, her neighbor, was her closest friend now. She had entrusted Nicky's care to her for a lot of years while she was working. She would talk to Beth and seek out her advice.

On the advice of Isaac Steinberg, her investment counselor, Vickie called Gregory O'Toole, an attorney who specialized in estate planning. Mr. O'Toole had his office in Eugene but was willing to drive to Florence to meet with Vickie.

On a Wednesday morning in the first week of October, Gregory O'Toole pulled up in front of Vickie Roberts' home in Florence. He noticed that it was a very nice home about five blocks back from the beach. It didn't look like it had any damage from the tsunami. He drove down to Front Street before he stopped at the Roberts' home and was dismayed at the destruction that was still evident around the area.

Vickie answered the doorbell when Gregory rang it. She was very nervous but knew that she must make sure her kids were taken care of.

"Thank you for coming all the way to Florence, Mr. O'Toole. My children are in school, and I can't be away from town for very long," Vickie explained.

"I completely understand, and it is no problem for me to come here. I love the beach but am dismayed to see the destruction that the tsunami caused. Not many shops have rebuilt, it seems," Gregory answered, and Vickie led him to the dining room table.

"Would you like a cup of coffee, Mr. O'Toole?" Vickie asked as she indicated a chair for him to sit down in.

"That would be very nice. Just black, please. And please call me Greg. Mr. O'Toole is my father, and it sounds strange for someone to call me that," Greg countered.

Greg opened a notebook to a blank sheet of paper and asked, "What can I do for you, Mrs. Roberts?"

"My name is Vickie," she said as she proceeded to explain to Greg O'Toole her situation. She told him about her parents being killed when she was 18, about inheriting this house and a fairly decent estate from them, about meeting and marrying Dan, about the lumber yard, the cabin in the woods, about the kids, and the fact that Nicholas was a special needs child, and even about Nick's sand dollar business. She was exhausted when she was finished.

"Vickie, it sounds to me like you need to have your will revised and new directives drawn up. You also need to have your money placed into a trust for your children so that if something happens to you before they reach majority, they are protected and the money is used for their care and education," Gregory explained. "Do you have someone specific that you know will take care of your kids?"

"Yes. I have talked to my neighbors Beth and Ralph Freeman. They have one boy the same age as Nick. Ralph is a vet, so they make a fairly decent living. And Beth has taken care of Nick for years while I was working. I was the head cashier at the grocery store, but after the tsunami, George Barnes had to put us all on furlough because he couldn't pay us with no money coming in. At that time, Dan and I decided that we would take a monthly income from our investments and I could stay home with the kids. We felt it wasn't fair to Maggie to have to take care of Nick every Saturday while Dan and I worked," Vickie felt deflated after she made this announcement to Greg. She thought it was so sad that she had no one but a neighbor to take care of her kids if she was gone. Thank God she had some money to support them.

"Do you intend to keep this house?" Greg asked.

"Heavens yes! This is my home. It was my parents' home, and I inherited it when they died. There is no mortgage on it, and Dan was able to keep up the maintenance and add some additions on as the kids grew," Vickie explained.

"What about the cabin? Will you keep that?" Greg continued to question Vickie about her assets.

"Yes. Right now, I have no intention of getting rid of it. That was our retreat and summer vacation site for years," Vickie stated very firmly. "We had made plans to run an additional electrical line in and add a refrigerator. Dan had all of the supplies, but we didn't find the time to get up there so he could do the work."

"Okay, Vickie. I think I have all of the information that I need for now. I will make a rough draft of what I think you want and need as far as your will and directives are concerned. Shall we make an appointment for next week? I really do not mind coming out here. Anywhere along the Oregon Coast is my happy place, and I take every opportunity I can to come here," Greg explained.

After Greg O'Toole left, all Vickie wanted to do was crawl into bed and sleep, but sleeping was hard without Dan lying next to her.

# CHAPTER 11

───────◆·•◆•·◆───────

Whenever Maggie could, she took Nicky down to the beach to look for sand dollars. It wasn't very often that they came home empty-handed. Most of the time, they found at least three or four good shells. It was a great day when they found eleven of them.

Both Maggie and Nicky missed Dan's presence in the house. Nick kept saying that he wished his dad would come home. Vickie was worried about him because he didn't seem to be mourning his dad. She decided to talk to the school counselor to see if he needed some individual counseling.

Maggie seemed to be even more patient with Nicky now than she was before Dan died. She was acting like she was responsible for Nick now. She had become more attentive to Nick's needs and seemed to become more remote where Vickie was concerned. She didn't initiate conversations with her and only gave brief answers to questions that Vickie would ask her.

Maggie had a birthday coming up in a month, and Vickie asked her what she would like to do. She could have a party at the house, or they could have a pizza party somewhere. She threw out another possibility of going to the cabin.

"Mom, I just want to spend the day with my friends. I don't need some kind of kids' party. That would be really lame, and I do not want to go to the cabin," she announced firmly.

"Maggie, Nick, and I would like to celebrate your birthday with you. Your friends could come here. We don't need to have a party, just snacks and maybe a birthday cake," Vickie suggested.

"Thanks anyway, Mom, but I just want to spend the day at Jeannie's house."

"Nicky will be very disappointed," Vickie stated matter-of-factly.

"I will explain it to him, Mom. Don't worry," Maggie said to her mother as she was walking out the door to go to Jeannie's house.

Nick came into the kitchen from the patio looking for Maggie. "Where is she, Mom?" he asked. "I need her to spray the sealer on my finished sand dollars. Mr. Barnes needs them as soon as possible so he can sell them."

"Honey, I'm sorry, but she has gone over to Jeannie's house," Vickie announced. "But maybe I can help. I can probably handle a spray can."

"Okay, Mom, but you have to be very careful not to get the sealer on anything else," Nick explained.

"How about if I read the directions on the can first? Maybe that will help me do a good job."

"Okay, Mom, but let's get with it. I need to have these done fast," Nick announced as he led Vickie onto the back patio.

Vickie laughed at her son and followed him out to the patio. He had lined up ten sand dollars that he had painted, all a little different from the others and, Vickie thought, absolutely beautiful. His work had improved so much since he had first started painting sand dollars.

"Here, Mom. Here's the can of sealer. All you have to do is put an even layer of sealer over each sand dollar. Maggie says if you get too much, it will make the painting look blurry, but if you don't get enough, it will not seal right. I will watch you do it for the first time and make sure you can do it right."

Vickie took the spray can and put an even coat of sealer over each of the sand dollars, and Nick agreed that she had done a good job. Since the weather was mild, he decided to leave them on the table to dry and not move them. The sealer was quick-drying, so they should be okay to move by evening.

"I wish we had an extra room for my sand dollars, Mom. It would be easier, and then I could paint them during the cold weather. Did you know that I can look for sand dollars all year long? A lot of them are on the beach after a storm. Maggie told me that. It would really be nice to have an extra room, wouldn't it?" Nicky said with a tone of pleading in his voice.

"It sure would, Nick!" Vickie stated. "Then I could come out onto the deck to have my lunch."

"Maybe Dad could—oh, I forgot, Dad isn't coming around anymore," Nick said very quietly.

Vickie put her arms around her son and quietly cried for him, for Dan, and for Maggie and herself. "Nicky, it isn't that Dad doesn't want to come around anymore. He would love to be here with all of us all of the time, but Dad got very sick, very fast, and died. He can't come around anymore, but you can still talk to him. He can hear you, but he can't answer you now. Someday, you will hear his answers in your heart. I talk to him all of the time and hear him talk to me right here," Vickie said as she put her hand up to her heart.

Nick had tears running down his cheeks but said in a halting voice, "But your heart is not your ears, Mom. I really wish I could hear him."

"I do too, Nicky!" Vickie stated firmly to her son.

Vickie didn't notice, but Maggie and Jeannie were standing in the doorway listening to the conversation between Vickie and Nick. "I wish I could hear him too, Nicky, but maybe someday we will, the same way Mom does." She walked over to her mother and brother and gave them both a hug.

"Jeannie and I came home to let you know that we were going down to the beach and wondered if Nick would like to come along. Jeannie wants to know more about Nick's sand dollar business," Maggie announced.

"Can I please, Mom? There is a chance I can find some more sand dollars. I can always use more," Nick begged.

"Okay, but dinner will be ready in about an hour. Jeannie, would you like to stay?" Vickie asked. "We are having tacos."

"Thank you, Mrs. Roberts. I would love to stay," Jeannie answered.

Tacos were an easy meal for Vickie to fix. It took very little time to get everything cut up, cook and season the meat, and grate the cheese. It was a good, healthy meal, and the kids both liked them, so there were no complaints. Vickie didn't have to cook very much after Dan died. People kept bringing her casserole dishes of food. She hardly had room in her refrigerator for a quart of milk, let alone the gallon that she always bought. Both Nicky and Maggie complained about the kind of food and the amount of leftovers they were eating all of the time. There was enough food that she gave some to Beth and Ralph.

It was mostly people from the church who were bringing all the meals for her. She finally asked Rev. Silas to make an announcement that she didn't need all of the extra meals. Vickie wrote a thank-you note that was printed in the weekly newsletter that went out to all members of the congregation, and finally the food stopped coming. The kids were relieved that they were going to eat their mom's cooking again.

After Vickie did all of the preparation for dinner, she sat down to think about the need for extra room for Nicky's sand dollar business. They had no extra room in the house. They only had three bedrooms and no basement. She had a fairly good-sized garage, but it was full of boxes, yard tools, and extra yard furniture. She could just get her car in. Dan's truck sat outside at the edge of the driveway. The weather was going to get damp and cold very soon, which meant that Nick was going to have to suspend his painting until it cleared up in the late spring.

After dinner, Jeannie went home, Maggie went to her room to finish reading a book for her social studies class, and Nick went to his room to watch Superman or Batman or Spider-Man on TV. Vickie could never tell who they were. Nick liked them all.

She walked out onto the patio to look around the yard. It had become a habit since Dan died that she check to see that the yard gate was closed and latched and that Nick's sand dollars were all safe on the table. If the weather turned cold and wet, she would bring them in.

As Vickie was looking around the yard, she noticed the unused garden area in the corner and wondered if she could put a shed in that area for Nicky's sand dollar business. She had seen some very nice-looking sheds in the garden supply store parking lot. There were several different sizes, and it could be painted the same color as the house. Electricity would have to be put in for lights and heat, and she would probably have to have a water line for a sink. If she did that, her kitchen sink would not be all paint spattered. Between washing hands and paintbrushes, her sink was always multicolored. She had to scrub it out every night before fixing supper.

The next morning, after the kids went off to school, Vickie drove up the highway a couple of miles to Young's Garden and Feed Store. There weren't many flowers on display at this time of the year, but in another month, they would have Christmas trees for sale, and the parking lot and store would all be decked out for the holiday. Vickie looked at all of the sheds that were on display. There were six different sizes, some with workbenches and shelves already built in and some with just blank walls ready for the new owners to design what they wanted inside.

The owner of the store, Ed Parker, came out to see if Vickie needed any help in making her selection. She had pretty much made up her mind by the time he got there which one she wanted but had a lot of questions about adding electricity and plumbing to the shed once it was in place. She also wanted to know what kind of foundation the shed needed.

Ed Parker was a personable young man who had just taken over the business from his father the year before. His father had wanted to retire for some time and was waiting for Ed to know the business well enough to run it. So far, Ed was doing a good job. Profits had increased from the previous year, and the overall look of the store was more appealing to the customers.

"Hello, Mrs. Roberts," Ed greeted Vickie. Ed and his wife attended the United Methodist Church in town and knew Dan, Vickie, and the kids. "How are you doing?" he asked.

Vickie was so tired of people asking her that. How do they think she was doing after suddenly losing her husband? "I am doing fine, thank you, Ed. I am interested in putting a shed in my backyard so that Nicholas can do some artwork without making a mess of my patio and kitchen."

"Carol bought one of his sand dollars at the grocery store last week. They are really pretty. How large of a shed do you need?" Ed asked.

"I think this 10' by 10' one would be perfect for him. It already has the work table and shelves, but I need to know if water and electricity can be added. Also, should it be on a concrete foundation?" Vickie asked.

"Yes to all of them. It would be much better to be on a concrete pad. That way, you could insulate the floor to keep the shed warmer in the winter months. And yes, electricity is easy to put in. For water, you would need a water line either run from your house or from the street. That can run the cost up significantly," Ed explained. "And of course, everything has to be done to current code."

"Can you work up a bid for the entire thing for me? I don't want Nicky to have to suspend his painting in the winter because of the weather. Right now, he is working on the patio, but it will be too damp and cold for him soon," Vickie explained to Ed.

"Sure, I can work something up. I have both an electrician and a plumber that I work with. If you have someone else in mind, I can contact them for you," Ed said.

"No. Your recommendation will be fine. I don't know any plumbers or electricians. Thanks very much, Ed. I want to have this done as soon as possible. It feels like winter is coming on; I don't want Nick to have to stop. This little adventure of his is keeping him busy, and right now, that is what he needs. Let me know when you have a bid ready," Vickie said.

"Should be tomorrow, Mrs. Roberts," Ed answered as Vickie was heading for her car.

"And please call me Vickie," she hollered as she turned back and smiled.

There was one more thing that Vickie knew she had to face, and that was the lumber yard. She had only been out there once since Dan died, and she had been putting off dealing with the pain of being there and facing the decisions that had to be made, but it was time, so she decided to drive out there now.

As she drove into the yard, she had a sharp pain in her heart. She expected to see Dan standing there talking to Harry, his foreman, but

Harry was standing there talking to another of the workers. Harry saw her and came walking toward her car as she parked in front of the office.

"Hi there!" Harry said as he opened her door and helped her out of the car. "Good to see you, Vick. Come upstairs where it is quieter. What brings you here today?" Harry was afraid that Vickie was going to close the yard down, and he would lose his job. He couldn't afford to lose his job. He was getting married in a month and needed the income.

"It is time I deal with this," she said as she spread her arm out to indicate the lumber yard as a whole. "I cannot leave all of you in limbo any longer, not knowing what is going to happen to this business. Harry, I have to sell Roberts Lumber Yard. I cannot keep it as much as I would like to. It is too much of a reminder of Dan, and it hurts to even think about it, let alone come out here. And I know nothing about running a lumber yard or even running a business."

"Do you have a buyer?" Harry asked quietly.

"No. I don't even know how to go about advertising for a buyer. I am pretty sure there is no one around here who wants to buy a business like this. It is a pretty specialized business," Vickie added.

"I would like to buy it!" Ed blurted out.

"You want to buy the lumber yard?" Vickie asked incredulously. "Can you afford it?"

"No, not if you want to sell it outright and get all your money out right now. But if you would be willing to sell it on time with a personal contract, I could make monthly payments, probably for 100 years," Ed said with a smile on his face and a hint of sarcasm in his voice.

"I will have to think about that, Ed. I don't even know what the business is worth. I would have to have an appraisal done in order to set a fair price. And I will have to talk to my attorney about it," Vickie said.

"In the meantime, I know that Dan had a few personal things here in his office. I should probably clear them out," Vickie mentioned.

"I have not touched anything in his office except some bookkeeping papers that had to be handled for payroll. Everything is still the same," Ed said quietly. "I will get you some boxes to pack his stuff in."

"Thanks," Vickie said as she walked into Dan's office and closed the door behind her.

# CHAPTER 12

---

*V*ickie had a funny feeling in the pit of her stomach when she sat down at Dan's desk. She felt like she shouldn't be there and that she should not be delving into his private business, but she had every right, and she had to do it to have some kind of closure for the business. If she was going to sell it, she had to get his things out of the office.

She looked around at the office, noticing all of the personal touches he had added. There were pictures that the kids had drawn for him when they were very small. He had them pinned to the walls all around the office. Sitting on his desk was their wedding picture and a picture of the two of them at the cabin not long after they were married. She remembered that weekend. It was hard for her to think of it now. She missed his presence so much that it physically hurt her.

Harry knocked on the door, opened it, and put some cardboard boxes inside. "If you need help carrying them to your car, let me know and I will do it for you. Please don't feel you have to rush or finish it all in one day. No one will disturb the office," Harry reassured her.

"Thanks, Harry. I appreciate the time," Vickie responded.

She spent the next hour taking things off of the walls, bookshelves, and desk and packing them in boxes. Not only were there pictures from the kids, but there were also letters from members of the community thanking Dan for the load of firewood that he took to them when they couldn't afford to heat their homes. There were certificates of appreciation for contributions, both monetary and logs for different raffles and auctions that organizations in town were having. It seemed that Dan gave to all of them. There were snapshots of different people who came to the lumber yard for tours and a fairly large picture of kids from the Florence Elementary School who had come to the yard for a field trip.

Vickie knew nothing about any of these accolades that Dan received. He never talked about any of it. Vickie never came to the office and never saw any of the certificates or pictures. She vowed right then that she would put all of this into a scrapbook someday for Maggie and Nicholas. They needed to be aware of what their father had done for his town and the people who lived in it. No wonder so many people showed up at his funeral.

Harry carried the filled boxes to Vickie's car. She let him know that she would be back in a couple of days to finish the job and that she would arrange for an appraisal of the yard and its equipment— talk to her attorney and possibly set a purchase price within a couple of weeks.

All of the boxes were piled into the garage until she could figure out how she was going to proceed with making a scrapbook out of most of the material in them. It was very important to Vickie that her children know what a special and unique man their father was.

When Vickie went back to the yard to finish cleaning out Dan's office, she found one of Nicky's painted sand dollars sitting on the back of the toilet in the bathroom. It was sitting on a note that Nick had written to his dad.

"Dad," the note started in Nick's funny handwriting. "I made this sand dollar especially for you. I remember finding one of my first sand dollars when you took me to the beach early one Saturday morning when Mom and Maggie were still asleep. And I remember that we both peed in the ocean. I thought it was so funny. You told me it was okay if I peed in the ocean—that no one would see me. And to prove it, you peed too. Thanks, Dad. You made me feel better that day."

Vickie sat there and cried for all Nicky would miss in the years to come and for all Dan would miss in not seeing his son grow. Nick might be a special needs child, but he gave so much to everyone who knew him, and Dan knew that. She lovingly wrapped the sand dollar along with the letter and set it aside to carry it to the car herself. All of his sand dollars reflected his special talent, but this one was special and meant the world to her. She would treasure it always.

Vickie talked to the owners of the Florence Lumber Mill about selling Dan's business. They were very sorry that she had to sell but understood that it was for the best. The owner said that he could arrange for a professional to give her an appraisal on the value of the yard, the equipment, and the contracts that Dan had negotiated with different mills around the area, including his own. They all would be considered in setting a price for the business.

In the meantime, Ed Parker had called Vickie to let her know that he was mailing her a bid on the shed along with the foundation, water, and electricity needed to fulfill all of her needs. He also had recommendations for two people who could do the work. They were both licensed and bonded and would do a very good job for her. He also assured her that it could be done with no delay, but the concrete foundation would have to be poured soon so that it could dry and cure before the building was put onto it and anchored down.

When Vickie received the proposed bid, she was a little surprised at the cost but felt that it would be worth it in the long run. The concrete pad and anchoring the shed to it were just about as expensive as putting a water line to it. The water line would have to come from the street and not from the house, which was farther and would necessitate digging up a portion of her yard. She wasn't too happy about that, but again, decided that it would be worth it in the long run. She didn't want to say anything to Nick yet but thought that she might tell Maggie what her plans were and get her input.

When Maggie and Nick got home from school, Nick went into his room to do his homework. He had some arithmetic problems he had to do. It was very hard for him, but he knew he had to get it done before he could work on his sand dollars. Mom said he couldn't touch them until she checked his work, and Mom was strict about homework. Dad was too, but Dad wasn't around to check it anymore.

"Maggie, would you come and sit with me for a minute? I need to ask you something," Vickie called out to her daughter.

"Did I do something wrong?" asked Maggie.

"Of course not. I just want to talk to you about a plan I have been working on," answered Vickie.

Maggie was a little nervous as she sat down at the kitchen table with her mother. Vickie told Maggie about the shed and what it would be used for. She told her about putting electricity and heat in it and about plumbing for a sink.

"Maggie, it will tear up the backyard for a while, and I might need your help putting things back together and planting flowers again in the spring. I don't know how deep they will have to go, but the temperature rarely goes below freezing, so they shouldn't have to dig too far down."

"Mom, that is a terrific idea. I would love to ask some of my friends to come over, but the patio is always a mess with Nick's sand dollars. I love him doing them, and the fact that he can sell them, but they are a mess. And yes, I will help you plant again in the spring if I can help you choose the flowers to plant," Maggie announced.

Very much relieved that Maggie approved of her idea, Vickie told her she could pick all of the flowers if she wanted to.

The men came to put the frame up for the cement foundation. They leveled the ground and laid the boards in. Then the cement truck came and poured the cement into the frame. That part of the project was finished when Nick and Maggie got home from school. Since they went into the house through the front door and up to their rooms to do homework, they did not see what was going on in the backyard.

"Hey Mom!" Nick yelled from his bedroom. "Someone has made a mess of the backyard." As soon as he said it, he ran into the kitchen and out onto the patio to check on his sand dollars. He was afraid that whoever messed up the backyard might have done something bad to his paintings.

"It's okay, Nick. I am having a special place put in the corner of the yard for you to paint your sand dollars. You will not have to do them on the patio anymore. You will have a room of your own with lights, a heater, and even a sink with running water so that you can wash your brushes and your hands and not get the kitchen sink dirty," Vickie explained to her astounded son.

"A place all my own?" Nick asked, wide-eyed.

"Yes, but Maggie and I will be able to come in to see how you are doing and help you once in a while."

"Gee, Mom! That's great. When will it be done so I can move in? Will I have my bed in there and my TV?" Nick asked.

"No, definitely not. You will still sleep in your bedroom and watch your programs in there or in the living room with Maggie and me. This room will be just for your painting," Vickie explained. "It should be ready for you to move all of your painting supplies and sand dollars into it in about two weeks."

The weather turned cold, rainy, and windy. Nick could not work on his sand dollars outside, and it took longer than expected for the concrete to settle and cure. After two weeks, the shed was delivered, only for Vickie to realize that it was not the one she had ordered and had to be returned. In the meantime, the contractor for the plumbing had started digging up the yard for the water line. Because of the rain, the yard was a muddy mess, and Nicky was upset because he could not work on his sand dollars.

It took another week for Ed Parker to get the right shed delivered to Vickie's property. "I am very sorry, Vickie. I have no control over the manufacture of the shed," Ed explained.

"I know, Ed, it is not your fault, but it is very frustrating anyway. It is like putting together a puzzle. When one piece doesn't fit properly, the whole puzzle doesn't come together. Nicky is frustrated because he can't work on his sand dollars, and when Nicky is frustrated, the whole household suffers," Vickie explained.

Finally, the shed arrived, was put together, and anchored to the concrete foundation, and the plumbing was completed with a sink installed. Now it was time for the electricity to be hooked up. Vickie was very particular about the type of heat that was installed. She did not want a heater that something could be pushed up against and start a fire. Nick wasn't always aware of safety, and Vickie wanted to make sure that he and the property were safe, so a heater with a thermostat was installed so that it would turn off when it got to a certain temperature.

Finally, the interior of the shed was ready to paint. Nick, Maggie, and Vickie decided to do the job themselves. The additional time spent, the upgraded heating system, and an upgrade in the sink style had all cost more money, so anything that they could do themselves was a plus for Vickie's pocketbook. Nick wanted the colors for the interior of his room to be the same colors that he painted his sand dollars. Both Vickie and Maggie weren't sure about how it would look but were surprised at the finished walls. The shelves and workbench were all covered with oilcloth so that they would be easy to clean, and linoleum was put onto the floor, again for ease of cleaning.

Nicky had gotten a cold the week before move-in day and had spent two days out of school and in bed. Vickie was exhausted from trying to supervise the construction and painting and keeping Nicky down and resting. He was running a fever but wanted to be outside watching his building. The weather was not clearing up, and the wind was causing high waves to come up onto the beach. There were some waves that came as far as the seawall. The town had shored up the seawall after the last high wave and was confident that, barring another tsunami, it would hold the water from crossing Front Street.

In the meantime, it caused Nick some major frustration because his mother would not let him go to the beach to look for more sand dollars. Maggie had bundled up and gone down a couple of times, but it was cold and windy, and she was uncomfortable. She did not want to get a cold too.

# CHAPTER 13

Nicky was sick over Thanksgiving, and Vickie downplayed the holiday. These first holidays without Dan were going to be hard on the family. They would have to make new traditions. They usually went to the cabin for Thanksgiving and for a few days during the Christmas break from school, but Vickie and Maggie didn't want to go this year. Nicky was disappointed that they were not going and couldn't understand the reason why they were not. He still hadn't grasped the idea that his dad was not ever coming back.

One of their traditions was to go to the cabin and tromp around in the woods to find their Christmas tree. This year, Vickie had decided to buy one from Ed Parker's Garden and Feed Store. Nicky was angry that they didn't go to the woods to cut one down and refused to help decorate the one they bought. Maggie was sad too, but understood why her mother did not want to go up and cut one themselves.

Vickie and Beth Freeman had made a trip to Newport before Thanksgiving to do their major Christmas shopping, and Beth had taken both Maggie and Nick out by themselves to shop for their mother, but none of the Roberts family was enthusiastic about the holiday this year.

Finally, during the second week of December, Nick's shed was complete and ready for move-in day. That caused more excitement for all three of them than Christmas did this year.

Nick was very specific about where he wanted everything to go. "Mom, I have drawn out this plan," he said as he showed both Vickie and Maggie his roughly drawn plan of shelves and a work table and where he wanted everything to be placed. "See, Mom, the color of the shelf is where I want that color of paint to go. Isn't that clever of me, Mom?" Nick looked up at her with bright eyes. He wasn't completely over his cold yet and was bundled up in a coat, scarf, and hat, and looked so sweet supervising move-in day. Vickie couldn't help smiling at him, even though she was tired and very sad that Dan could not be there to enjoy this time with his son.

Nicky was thriving in his new room. He called it his studio. He had heard the word on a TV program pertaining to an artist working in his studio, so that is what his room became—Nick's Studio.

Maggie was loving school this year. Since she wasn't in the lowest grade level in high school, she felt a little more important. Her grades were good, and she was taking an interest in her math classes. Her beginning algebra class was fascinating to her, and she was surprised at how much algebra was used in daily life.

"Mom, did you realize that you use algebra when you cook?" she asked Vickie.

"How do I use algebra? I never liked it in school," Vickie answered, smiling at her daughter.

"Mom!" Maggie said, exasperated. "When you double a recipe, like you do cookies when you bake them (hint, hint), you use algebra to double the measurements of the ingredients."

"Gee, I didn't know that. Maybe I learned something in high school after all," Vickie teased her daughter.

"I like math. I might take more math classes next year. My grades are good in math too. Mom, sometimes I think that Dad is up there telling me that I can do whatever I want to and I will be good at it.

It is like he is encouraging me all of the time. Is it weird to feel that way?" Maggie asked.

"No, it isn't. I feel that way about Dad too. I think he is telling us that it is okay to make mistakes once in a while, but as long as we learn from them and don't make the same mistake again, we are doing good. He is watching out for us," Vickie said quietly.

"Hi! Whatcha talking about?" Nick asked as he bounded into the room.

Maggie laughed at the look on her brother's face when she told him that they were talking about how much she liked math. "Ugh! I sure don't like it. In fact, I think I might quit school. I have a business now and a studio to work in. Maybe I will retire and paint sand dollars for a living."

Both Maggie and Vickie burst out laughing. "Sweetheart, I don't think you are making quite enough money yet to support yourself. You have to stay in school. Do you know that it is the law that you go to school? They could put me in jail if you decided to quit now," Vickie explained to Nick.

"Gosh, I wouldn't want that. You are the only one who knows how to cook. Maggie is terrible at it!" he announced. They laughed even louder. Maggie agreed with him.

"Stay in school, Nick. We need Mom around to cook for us!"

It had only been a few months since Dan had died, and Vickie still hurt all of the time, but she was beginning to laugh again. If they could laugh at each other like they just had, maybe they would be okay after all.

Nick went back to his painting, Maggie went to her room to finish her homework, and Vickie started dinner for her family.

Vickie wondered what she was going to do for the rest of her life now that Dan was gone. Nick would probably always need her around, but Maggie was growing up and, in a couple of years, would be off to college. She needed something to keep her occupied. She had thought about talking to George Barnes about going back to the grocery store on a part-time basis. She would need to be home when Nick got home from school, but then she thought about being on her feet all of the time and decided that it wasn't for her. What was she going to do?

She had decided to go to the women's luncheon at church on a Wednesday. She hadn't been to one since Dan had died. It was too hard answering everyone's prying questions, but she thought that it would do her good to get out of the house and be around some other women for a change.

Shirley Parker, Ed's wife, was there and was asking her how the new shed was working out for her. Almost all of the ladies at the luncheon knew about Nick's painted sand dollars and were interested in the new shed that she had put up in the backyard.

"You know, it is working out very well. Nick is thriving in his 'Studio,' as he calls the shed. I love the fact that all of the mess is out there and not in my kitchen sink. George Barnes is doing a good job of selling the sand dollars, and Nick is really loving watching his savings account grow. He told Maggie and me the other day that he thought he would quit school now. He was making some money and didn't have to go to school," Vickie explained to all of the ladies. They all laughed at what Nick had said.

"What are you doing now, Vickie, to fill your days? You must be at loose ends," Cindy Horton-Silas said. Cindy was Pastor Jim Silas' wife and was the organizer of the women's luncheons.

"I am! I have been trying to think of something to do to keep me busy when the kids are in school. I thought about asking George for a part-time job at the grocery, but the thought of being on my feet all of the time discouraged me from asking."

"Vickie, you are an excellent seamstress," said Susan Henderson, Jeannie's mother. "I have seen some of the clothes you make for Maggie, and they are very professional looking. Have you thought of doing sewing as a profession?"

The other ladies were nodding their heads in agreement. "That's a great idea, Vickie. You are a very accomplished seamstress," someone else said.

"I really haven't thought about it. I have only made clothes for Maggie and myself. I have made the occasional shirt for Nick, but that is about all," Vickie answered.

Vickie drove to the church for the luncheon, and as she was driving home, she stopped at the only store in town that sold fabric and sewing notions. She could only take a minute in the store to look around. The kids were due home from school in a short time.

Maybe she could do some sewing for other people. She didn't know who would want to buy her creations, but she might try. She knew that she would need a better sewing machine if she was going to do professional sewing. Hers was just a basic machine and was her mother's, so it was pretty old. It still worked for what she did now, but it probably would not hold up under more constant use. Maybe it was time to make a trip to Eugene to the fabric store and look around there.

She would ask Beth if she could keep Nick on Saturday. He would absolutely not enjoy wandering around a fabric store with her and Maggie. He wouldn't be happy about not being in his studio, but he would have to put up with it. She had put a key lock on the door so he could not be in there without her knowing about it. The door was locked when they were not at home, and she always locked it at night.

Beth agreed to keep Nick for the day and to take him to the beach to look for sand dollars while she and Maggie went to Eugene. Beth had already put an order in for a new dress for her wedding anniversary in the summer. It would be her 10th, and she and Ralph were going to celebrate.

So, on Saturday morning, Nick grudgingly went to Beth's, angry at his mom for not letting him into his studio, and Maggie and Vickie were off on their adventure to Eugene in search of a new sewing machine.

Before Vickie had made up her mind to buy a new machine, she had checked with Isaac Steinberg about her investments. She wanted to make sure that what she spent was not going to cut into her savings drastically.

"Vickie, if you are going to start a business, any investment you make in equipment for that business will be a write-off on your taxes, so you shouldn't worry about whether you can afford it. Even if you do not make a business out of your sewing, you certainly can afford a new sewing machine. You and Dan did a good job of setting up your estate. You do not need to worry, and if things get to the point where I think you should begin to worry, I will let you know," Isaac explained to her. "Anyway, Annie wants to order a new dress from you. She is always complaining that she has to go so far to get any good quality clothing."

"Thank you, Isaac. I just want to make sure that I am not cutting into any funds that the kids will need. I guess I don't need the extra money that I would make from sewing. I just need something to keep me busy when the kids are in school," Vickie responded quietly.

"Go and have fun with your daughter and don't worry!" Isaac reassured her.

The drive to Eugene was uneventful. She and Maggie talked about events at school and at church. Maggie brought up the fact that it was about time for her to take traffic safety and get her learner's permit so that she could learn to drive. Vickie was really dreading that. It scared her to think that her daughter would be out on the road driving. It was a young boy who had just gotten his driver's license a week before that caused the accident that killed her parents. Maggie's driving was not a subject she wanted to think about, let alone talk about.

"I will think about it, Maggie, but I would prefer that you wait a while longer before you get your license. I have told you about my parents' accident. I don't want anything happening to you," Vickie explained her hesitancy.

"Mom, that was a long time ago, before they had traffic safety classes in the schools. The instruction is a lot better now. Please, Mom, think about it. I will be 16 in October, and I don't want to be the only one in my class who doesn't have a license," Maggie begged.

"I will think about it," Vickie reassured her daughter.

Vickie and Maggie walked into the fabric store. The store had a limited variety of sewing machines, and they were very expensive. They looked at all of them, but Vickie wasn't pleased with the price of any of them.

She knew that in the mall, there was a sewing machine and vacuum cleaner shop, so she and Maggie went there. They had a huge inventory of machines to choose from, and the prices were about $100.00 less expensive across the board than the ones in the fabric store.

A very nice and knowledgeable gentleman was helping them. He explained the functions of the machines that Vickie was interested in and didn't try to push her into purchasing a more expensive machine.

She settled on a new Viking machine. It had all of the functions that she wanted and was listed at a price she thought was fair for the type and quality of machine.

Maggie was looking at a serger while Vickie was paying for the machine. She wanted to purchase an additional warranty that would add to the limited warranty that came with the machine, and it was taking a little longer than she had expected.

"Mom, look at this. It finishes the seams on a dress so they don't ravel. Some of the blouses that you have given me had seams that are finished like this. It is cool."

The salesman had finished the paperwork on the additional warranty, got up from his chair, and walked over to hand Vickie her receipt. He was ready to carry the machine out to her car for her. "Are you interested in a serger?" he asked.

"I hadn't thought about it until my daughter pointed out that it does make the garments look more professional," Vickie mentioned.

Vickie wound up buying the serger also. She had never used one before and would have to learn how, but knew she could. She was excited about launching a new business. She kind of knew how Nicky felt when he started painting his sand dollars and selling them to George Barnes.

Vickie had not thought ahead about where she was going to do her sewing. She did not have an extra room to convert into a sewing room and didn't really want everything on her dining room table, although she had not used it since Dan died. That did not mean she would not use it at some time. When she sewed for Maggie, she usually put up a card table in a corner of her bedroom, but she knew that a card table would not be enough room for both a sewing machine and a serger.

The lot that Vickie's house was on was large. It had been three city lots put together when her parents had bought it years ago, and they had the foresight to build their home on the westernmost side of the property. Most of the area was planted in grass, and with Dan gone, she had to hire someone to mow it. Nicky was too young to handle the mower, and she wasn't sure she would trust him if he was old enough.

She was standing at the far eastern side of her property, looking at her house and the area around it, and wondering if it would be possible to add another room off of her bedroom. It would really be incredible to have the extra space for sewing. It would give her more storage also. She thought that an extra room would increase the value of the house too.

"I wonder!" Vickie said out loud. "I wonder if it would work. Maybe I need to get someone to look at the house and draw up some plans, but who do I get?"

She went back into the house to have a cup of coffee and think about what was happening in her life right now when the phone rang, and it was Harry Young, the foreman at the lumber yard. "Oh darn," she thought. "I haven't made a decision on whether I will be willing to hold the contract on the sale of the mill."

"Hello, Harry. How are you?" Vickie said when Harry identified himself. "I am sorry that I have not gotten back to you regarding the sale. A lot has been going on around here." Vickie hesitated for a moment, then said, "Yes, I will hold the contract for you at the price we talked about. I will call my attorney right now to draw up a contract of sale. It shouldn't take him more than a week to get it to me, and I will get it to you for your attorney to review. Is that okay with you?" Vickie asked.

"That would be fine, Vickie, and thank you."

# CHAPTER 14

*V*ickie made an appointment with Greg O'Toole to come to Florence on Friday to talk about the contract of sale for the Roberts Lumber Yard. She had a knot in her stomach the whole time she was talking to him. It was going to be very hard to sign an agreement to sell the yard. It was like losing Dan all over again, but she knew that she couldn't keep the yard. She knew nothing about running that type of business.

Greg arrived at Vickie's home on Friday at 10:00 AM, right at the agreed-upon time. Greg got the name and address of Harry's attorney and explained to Vickie that he would work directly with him. He would draw up a contract and send it to Harry's attorney for approval. If it was approved, they would set up a time when all four of them could meet so that the contract could be signed and witnessed. Greg wanted to make sure that everything was done legally and that in the future, nothing could come up to dispute the sale. Vickie would receive a monthly payment of the loan, and it would be sent directly to her bank. She would not have to deal with a check and making a deposit herself.

"Peter, can I fix you some lunch while you are here? It is a long drive for you to make, and I don't want you to go away hungry," Vickie offered.

"No thanks, Vickie. I have a 1:00 appointment and need to get back to the office to prepare for it. I will grab something on the way back. I will call you and let you know when the papers are ready, and we will set up an appointment with Harry's attorney. Since he is local, I will come here. Like I said before, I will take any opportunity I can to come to the beach, even if it is just to drive to the end of the road and look at the ocean for a few minutes, which is what I will do before heading home. Thanks for the lunch offer. Maybe next time," Greg explained.

When Greg left, Vickie called Harry at the yard and explained to him what was going to happen next and that his attorney would be contacting him.

"Thanks, Vickie. I am excited about purchasing the business. By the way, I intend to keep the 'Roberts Lumber Yard' name. I will just advertise that it is under new management," Harry explained.

"Thanks! That is very kind of you, Harry. See you soon," Vickie said quietly as she hung up the phone, sad that she was going to sell the yard. It was like the last vestige of Dan was going to be leaving her.

Vickie was sad for a couple of days, but soon put the sale to the back of her mind and concentrated on the addition she wanted to put onto the house. She had talked to both Maggie and Nick about the new room, and they thought it was a great idea.

"Mom, you and I can have our businesses together. Maggie, you need to start a business. Then we would all have jobs to do," Nicky announced to his sister.

"I have enough of a job concentrating on my schoolwork. I want to go to college and study math, and I need to keep my grades up if I want to get into a good college. Mom, I'm thinking about Stanford. What do you think?" Maggie asked.

"I'm not sure I like the idea of you being so far away, but I know it is one of the best schools on the West Coast, and it would be a great experience for you. Let's see how things go. You can apply to as many schools as you want. I would prefer that you stay on the West Coast, but that is up to you," Vickie said, dreading the day when Maggie would actually leave home. She knew that when she left home for college, she would probably not come back home to live for very long. She knew that the college experience and the independence that it provided young people changes them, and she knew that it would happen to Maggie too.

"This is a boring conversation, Mom," Nick announced. "The thought of all that math hurts my head. May I be excused, please?" Nick asked.

Both Vickie and Maggie laughed at the face that Nick made when he said the word "math." Nick did not like math at all and dreaded that time of day when he had to do it in school. He struggled with all of his schoolwork, but math was the worst.

"Yes, you may be excused, but you must bring me your homework so I can review it with you," Vickie said.

"Oh, Mom!" Nick moaned.

"Those are the rules, Nick. You know that you cannot work on your sand dollars until your homework is finished and finished correctly," she admonished him.

Nick went off to his room to get his homework to show his mother. "I feel so sorry for him sometimes, Mom. I have tried to work with him on his numbers, but he just doesn't grasp the concept of arithmetic, and I don't know what else to do to help him," Maggie explained to her mom.

"I know, honey, and I appreciate you trying to help him. I fear that he will never really grasp the concept of math. He doesn't do much better with his reading either, although he read me a couple of pages in one of his books the other day," Vickie said. "But he really struggles."

Nick came out of his room with his math paper. It was crumpled and messy. Vickie admonished him for the way it looked. "Nick, you must take more pride in all of the work you do. You are so careful with the painting you do on your sand dollars, but your school papers are a mess," she told him.

"Mom, I get so frustrated. I don't understand this stuff at all. I don't know why I have to do it at all. It isn't ever going to do me any good," Nick cried. He sat down with a plop and put his head down on his chest.

"Nick, I have told you before that you will need to know math so that you can figure out if you are being paid the right amount for your sand dollars. You will need to be able to figure out how much each sand dollar is worth, and you will need to know how much you can spend on your paint and supplies," Vickie explained to him again.

"I thought you would do that for me, Mom," Nick stated.

"Maybe I won't be around to do it for you. When you get older, you will be able to walk to the store by yourself. Then you will have to know all of this," Vickie explained again.

Nick stood up and stomped out of the room. "Nicholas!" Vickie called him back. He stopped, turned around, and looked at his mother. "Please do this paper over so that your teacher will be able to read it. No painting sand dollars until I approve it. Do you understand?"

"Yes, Mom!" Nickie answered in a sullen voice.

Vickie was concerned about Nick's attitude. She wondered if something happened at school to make him act the way he was about his schoolwork. He had always had a hard time with his studies, but at least he tried. Now it seemed that he wasn't even trying. She was going to call Mrs. Carpenter, Nick's teacher, and set up an appointment for a conference. She knew that teacher conferences were coming up next month, but she wanted to get on top of the problem right now.

Vickie called the school and made an appointment with Nick's teacher for Thursday after school. Just as she hung up, Nick and Maggie walked in the door, ready for a snack and to do their homework. Vickie had baked some cookies that morning, and a plate of them was sitting on the kitchen table. Nick grabbed three cookies and headed for his room without any comment to his mother. Maggie held back to speak to her mom. "Mom, he was crying when I picked him up. That is not the first time I have seen him crying after school, but he won't tell me what's wrong. He just runs ahead."

"I have noticed that his homework is very sloppy, and sometimes his papers look like they are crumpled up. I have made an appointment with Mrs. Carpenter for Thursday after school. Will you be able to stay here with him while I am gone? I would like to find out what, if anything, is going on at school that would upset him," Vickie asked.

"Sure, Mom. I will be here," Maggie said as she picked up a cookie and went to her room to do her homework.

Vickie knocked on Nick's bedroom door and walked in. Just then, he was crumpling up his paper, obviously frustrated because he couldn't do or didn't want to do the homework. "What's wrong, Nick?" Vickie asked as she walked over to him.

"I don't see why I have to do this stupid math. I don't understand it, and I can't do it. I am just stupid anyway," Nick stated.

"Nicholas, you are not stupid, and don't let me ever hear you say that about yourself again," Vickie demanded.

"Everyone says I am. I can't do the same work as they do, and anyway, they say my dad even thought I was stupid. That's why he isn't here anymore. Mom, does Dad think I am stupid? Is that why he doesn't come home anymore?" Nick said with a longing look in his eyes.

"Oh, Nicky," Vickie cried as she gathered her son into her arms. "No, sweetheart. Your dad thought you were perfect just the way you are. He got very sick and died, Nick. That's why he isn't here now. Honey, always remember, your dad loved you very much. He wanted everything for you and would be here in a flash if he could. He was so proud of you and loved your painted sand dollars. He would be so proud that you are selling them."

"But I miss him, Mom!" Nick stated firmly. "I want him here now."

"I know, honey, I do too. So does Maggie, but it isn't possible. Dad's spirit is in heaven, but you know, you can talk to him anytime you want to. He can always hear you, and he will always listen," Vickie assured him.

Vickie went into her bedroom after she had left Nick. She sat on the edge of her bed and cried. "Oh, Dan, I need you so much. I don't know if I can do this by myself. Nick needs so much help right now, and Maggie needs your guidance. I am afraid I will not be able to be or do what they need. Please, Dan, ask God to give me the guidance that I need to raise these two precious beings in the manner that you would wish me to."

Just then, Maggie rapped on the door and walked into her mother's bedroom. "Mom, can I go over to Jeannie's house for supper? They are having tacos, and you know how I love tacos," Maggie asked. "Mom, what's wrong?" she asked when she saw her mother crying.

"Nothing, honey, just missing your dad," Vickie answered.

Maggie went to her mother and put her arms around her. "I miss him too, Mom – all of the time."

"Yes, you can go to Jeannie's if you have all of your homework done," Vickie smiled at her daughter. "I think I will take Nicky out for McDonald's. I am not on his good side right now and would like to get back there."

Maggie left to walk to Jeannie's house, and Vickie went into Nick's room to talk to him about dinner. "What would you like for dinner?" she asked.

"I'm not hungry now!" Nick mumbled, still angry at his mom for making him do his stupid math homework.

"Not even for McDonald's?" Vickie asked.

Nick brightened up a bit and looked at Vickie with a tear-stained face. "Can I have a Big Mac like Dad does?"

"Have you finished your math?" Vickie asked.

"Yes," Nicky said as he held up a rather messy paper for his mother's inspection.

"You got all of the answers correct, Nick. I am proud of you. We will have to work a bit on your neatness, but this is good. Yes, you can have a Big Mac. Give me about 15 minutes to get ready, and we will go. Maggie has gone to Jeannie's for supper, so it is just you and me tonight," Vickie said as she hugged Nicky's shoulders.

# CHAPTER 15

As Vickie was driving up to the elementary school for her conference with Mrs. Carpenter, Nicky's teacher, she was reflecting on the day she and Dan had first taken him to school. He had gone to preschool at their church for two hours a day but had not been away from them for the whole day. Both of them were nervous about his reactions but were very pleased that he took to it so well.

"Dan, I need your guidance today. Please be there for me," Vickie prayed as she parked the car and walked into the school.

"Hello, Mrs. Carpenter," Vickie greeted the teacher as she walked into the room. Joyce Carpenter was a young special education teacher just three years out of school. She had a master's degree in Special Education and was, according to all reports, one of the top special ed teachers in the State of Oregon. Why she remained in Florence, Oregon, was a mystery to her colleagues in the field.

"Hello, Mrs. Roberts. I hope you are well," Joyce Carpenter said as she motioned to a chair for Vickie to sit in.

"Thank you. I know that conferences are coming up in a couple of weeks, but I have some specific concerns about Nicky, and I wanted to get on top of them as soon as I could," Vickie explained. "Nicky has been more and more disinterested in his schoolwork lately. His work is sloppy, and it looks like he doesn't even try to do it correctly. I know he knows some of the math problems, but he doesn't seem to care, and I do not know what to do. All he wants to do is look for and paint his sand dollars. I don't know what to do for him to make him more motivated."

"Did you know that Nick has asked that he not be called 'Nicky' anymore?" Mrs. Carpenter asked.

"No! He hasn't said a word to me. When did he say this?" Joyce asked in a stunned voice.

"Last week. I asked him why, and he said that it made him sound like too much of a baby," she explained. "He seemed to indicate that some of the older boys had been teasing him about his name. I'm surprised he hasn't said anything to you."

"I am not his favorite person right now. We have a rule in our house that homework has to be done before any fun time. Nick wants to paint his sand dollars more than anything else, and I will not let him until he gets his work done. He thinks that is unfair. He told me a couple of weeks ago that he thought he might quit school and earn his living finding and painting his sand dollars," Vickie said with a chuckle in her voice. "I told him he has to go to school until he is 18 years old or graduates from high school. He did not like that one bit and has been giving me the cold shoulder ever since."

"He also mentioned to me that he was going to quit school. I told him I would be very sad not to have him in my classroom anymore, and I thought that he should stay in school for a while longer," Mrs. Carpenter added.

"Has he said anything about his dad to you?" Vickie asked.

"He did say that if his dad was here, he would let him quit school and even help him with his business because his dad was a businessman and knew what he was talking about," the teacher answered.

"He hasn't accepted the fact that his dad is dead. He hasn't ever had to face death before, even of a pet. We have never had one. He keeps telling me everything will be different when his dad gets home. I am stymied as to what to say to him," Vickie lamented.

"You might want to have him see a child psychologist. I am not sure if I would be qualified to address that issue," Mrs. Carpenter said.

"No, I am not asking you to. I just wanted your advice and input as to what's going on with him and to see if there is anything that I should be doing," Vickie explained.

"How is your daughter taking the death of her father?" Mrs. Carpenter asked.

"I think she is doing as well as can be expected. She has her friends to lean on, and we talk quite a bit about Dan and his hopes and dreams for both of them. She seems to accept the fact that he is gone. I guess it is hardest on me because I am dealing with all of this alone. It was not in my master plan," Vickie stated.

"It must be very daunting. All three of you might benefit from some counseling. It is nothing to be ashamed of, you know," Mrs. Carpenter mentioned.

"I have been thinking of it for myself, but have not figured out the logistics of it," Vickie mentioned. "I cannot leave Maggie in charge of Nick for any length of time if I am out of town, and there is no counselor here in Florence. I would have to go to either Lincoln City or Newport. I am not sure how Maggie would feel about going, but I would like to try. It might do us all good in different ways."

"I will not hold you up any longer, Mrs. Carpenter. Thank you so much for seeing me and for the advice. I will talk to Nick about the name change," Vickie said with a smile as she left the classroom.

"Oh, Mrs. Roberts, Nick's sand dollars are beautiful. He does a terrific job on them. I have bought a couple of them at the grocery store to give as gifts. I am impressed," Mrs. Carpenter said as Vickie was walking out.

"Thank you very much. I will tell Nick. He will be happy to hear that," Vickie said as she opened the door and left.

"Mom, do you think that if I prayed hard enough, Dad would come back?" Nick said at dinner after Vickie's meeting with her teacher.

"Sweetheart, I have told you that Dad will not be coming back. He is dead and in heaven. You learned about heaven in Sunday School. Dad is there with Jesus and with my mom and dad," Vickie tried to explain again.

"But I want him to come back here and live," Nick cried.

"Nick, Dad got very sick. His body couldn't get over the sickness, and he died," Maggie said. "Remember, you and I talked about it before. I would like him to come back too, and so would Mom, but he can't. Let's not upset Mom anymore by talking about him coming back."

Vickie looked at her daughter and wondered when she became so grown-up. "Thanks, Maggie," she said.

"Can I go out and paint on my sand dollars, Mom?" Nick asked.

"Sure, sweetheart. Want some help?" Vickie asked.

"No, I can do it," Nick answered as he left to run out to his studio. Vickie had had a sign made for his shed that said, "Sand Dollars by Nicholas," and Ralph Freeman had come over to hang it above the door of the shed. Nick said that the sign made him feel official.

After Nick had left the kitchen and Maggie was putting the dishes into the dishwasher, Vickie started talking to her about the possibility of all of them seeing a therapist.

"Mom, I don't need to see a shrink!" Maggie stated emphatically.

"I know, honey, but Mrs. Carpenter and I feel that Nick does, and she suggested we go as a family. It might help him to open up about Dad being gone. Nick does not accept the fact that he is dead, and both his teacher and I feel that he could use some professional help.

And did you know that he didn't want to be called 'Nicky' anymore?" Vickie asked.

"Yeah – he said something to me on the way home the other day. He gets teased when anyone calls him Nicky. Some of the older boys tease him and call him a baby. There have been several times that I noticed that he has been crying when I meet him at school to walk home. He won't tell me who they are, but I think I know. They bully a lot of the younger kids, especially the ones in special ed," Maggie explained. "And, yeah, Mom, I will go with you to a shrink as long as I don't have to bare my soul to him."

"You won't, unless you want to," Vickie answered with a smile on her face. Now the trick was to find one who would see them after school.

Vickie walked out to the shed to let Nick know that it was time to wrap things up and come in for his bath and to get ready for bed. As she walked into the shed, she saw Nick hunched over a sand dollar, putting the finishing touches on some lettering that he had done on it. She gasped when she saw that it said 'DAD' painted on a beautiful blue and yellow background that looked like a sunset over the ocean.

"Nick, that is beautiful," she praised him. "You have done a great job of painting that."

"I am going to give it to Dad when he comes back," Nick announced.

Vickie just looked at her son and wondered how soon she could find a therapist for the whole family.

On Friday, Vickie called Doc Jansen to make an appointment to see him. She wanted to ask him about a referral to a family therapist.

The weatherman had predicted a stormy weekend on the Northern Oregon Coast, and since Maggie had asked to spend Friday and Saturday nights with her friend Jeannie, Vickie decided that it would be fun to take Nick up the coast to look for sand dollars. It was easier to find them after a storm pushed them in to shore. She called Jeannie's mother to let her know that she would be away for Saturday and Sunday and then talked to Nick.

"How would you like to go on a little trip with me? I was thinking we would go up the coast to some of the beaches and look for sand dollars after the storm," Vickie asked.

"Oh, Mom, could we? I maybe could find a lot of them to paint," Nick responded with wide eyes.

"I think maybe you could. We would stay in a motel on Saturday night and get up very early Sunday morning to search the beach. Maybe we could drive up as far as Rockaway Beach. That is nice and flat and could have a lot of sand dollars. We could also scope out some of the gift shops along the way and see if they have any sand dollars for sale," Vickie added.

"What about Maggie, Mom? Would she come with us?" Nick asked about his sister.

"She has asked to stay with Jeannie for the weekend, so it would be just the two of us," Vickie explained.

"Ok! I have to go pack. I need a suitcase, Mom. Where is mine?" Nick asked.

"In the garage with all of the others. You don't need a very large one, Nick. We are only going for two days, but you will need a couple of changes of clothes in case you get wet. And be sure that you have your boots and warm socks. It will probably be raining. The weatherman has said we will have a stormy weekend. Let me check your bags before you close them up," Vickie instructed him.

"Are you sure you are okay with us leaving for the weekend?" Vickie asked Maggie when she came out of her room to help with supper.

"It's fine, Mom. It will be good for Nicky to have you to himself for a while. Jeannie and I are going to try to study for a big math exam. This exam will determine the math classes I take for the next two years. If I want to major in math in college, I have to take the right classes to prepare for it. Jeannie wants to major in both math and science, but I am not that interested in the science part of it. We might go to the beach if the weather is nice, or to a movie on Saturday night," Maggie explained to her mother.

"Well, if you need anything, Mrs. Henderson will help you or call Beth or Ralph next door. They are going to be around all weekend," Vickie assured her daughter.

# CHAPTER 16

Nick had always been an early riser, and this particular Saturday morning, he was up at 5:30 AM, already dressed in his beach combing clothes, including his boots. He walked into his mother's bedroom and announced in a fairly loud voice, "Ready to go, Mom!"

Vickie groaned, turned over, and looked at the clock and said, "Okay, Nick. Give me a few minutes to wake up, shower, get dressed, and fix some coffee for myself. We can stop and get some breakfast on the way. Would you please put your suitcase in the car? Also, make sure that you have enough bags to put the sand dollars in. I think it would be fun to separate them so that we know what beach they came from. Why don't you get 10 grocery bags and two felt markers? That way, we can mark the bags with the number of sand dollars in each and the beach that they came from," Vickie asked her son.

After her shower and a cup of coffee, Vickie and Nick finished loading the trunk of the car, locked up the house, and drove to McDonald's to get some breakfast to eat on the road. Vickie had decided late the previous evening to not only make this a fun trip with Nick, but to maybe help him understand math a little better. By counting the number of sand dollars they picked up, the number of beaches where they found them, and adding them up, he might learn to add a little better. Working with something he loved to do might encourage him. She hoped so.

The weather was not the best for beach combing, but Vickie and Nick made the best of it. Their first stop was Yachats, just a few miles up the coastline. Nick found four good sand dollars and Vickie found two. Nick instructed Vickie in how to place them in the bags so that they would not break and was very proud of the shells that they found. Vickie found a few other shells that were whole and very pretty and picked them up.

"Mom, you can't mix your shells with the sand dollars. We have to keep them separate. Here is another bag for yours," Nick told her as he pulled another plastic bag out of his coat pocket.

"Sorry, son. I forgot. Thanks for reminding me," she said with a big grin on her face.

After Yachats, they drove slowly up the coast, stopping in Newport at the grocery store to pick up a few things for lunch, then headed north again. Traffic was not at all heavy. The weather wasn't very conducive to a weekend at the beach for a lot of tourists. They saw a few RVs driving north, probably coming back from their winter in the south, but not a lot of traffic. Vickie was very glad of that. She was not really comfortable driving in heavy traffic.

They stopped at a few more beaches along the way and found several more sand dollars, and when they got to Tillamook, Nick wanted to tour the cheese factory. He loved to go in and taste all of the different kinds of cheese.

After the tour of the Tillamook Cheese Factory, they stopped at Rockaway Beach and found a treasure trove of sand dollars. Rockaway always seemed to be a good place to find shells. Nick also found a large glass float lying against an old log. He had never found a glass float before and was excited about his unusual find.

Vickie had decided that Cannon Beach was as far north as they would drive. They would find a motel room there and head back south in the morning.

They stopped to eat at a nice seafood restaurant, and Nick ordered his usual hamburger and fries. He lived at the beach, but the only kind of seafood he liked was crab, and that only if he could dig it out of the shells. The digging out was as much fun for him as eating it. Vickie ordered a cup of chowder and a plate of sea scallops. After a bowl of ice cream for Nick and a cup of coffee for Vickie, they headed back to the motel to count their sand dollars.

Vickie had Nick lay out each marked bag on the floor and removed the sand dollars from one bag at a time. Then she asked him to count each sand dollar in that bag and write it down on a piece of paper. He did this with each bag of sand dollars he had.

"Now, Nick, please add the row of sand dollars up so that you know how many you found today," she requested.

Nick looked at her with a blank face. "Why?" he asked.

"That is the only way to find out how many sand dollars you found today. You will need to know how many you found so that you can figure out how much paint you are going to need and how many cans of sealer you will need. In order to be able to make any money selling your sand dollars, you need to know how many you have to begin with and how much money you are going to spend getting them ready to sell. The cost of your supplies has to come off the total of dollars that you make. Then the difference is what you can put in the bank," Vickie carefully explained to Nick.

Nick looked at his mom for quite some time. She knew he was trying to process everything that she had said in his mind. All of a sudden, he got a big grin on his face and said, "I understand. If I am going to make any money, I have to subtract all of the money that I spend on paint, sealer, and brushes from the amount that Mr. Barnes gives me. That's simple, Mom!" Nick announced.

He got busy with his list of numbers and his pencil and concentrated for some time on the figures on the paper. It took him almost 30 minutes to come up with a total.

"I think this is right Mom, but will you please check it for me? I guess if I am going to own a business, I have to learn all of this stuff," Nick announced.

"I would be happy to check it for you, honey. I am very proud of you for figuring all of this out," Vickie said as she hugged her son and had a few tears in her eyes. She only wished that Dan could be here to see this breakthrough. But then, she thought that he probably was.

On their drive back down the Oregon Coast the next day, Vickie and Nick stopped at some different beaches to look for sand dollars. Since there had been a higher than normal tide the night before, there were quite a few whole sand dollars on the beaches, and again, Nick and Vickie picked up a load of them. Fortunately, Nick had stuffed a lot of plastic bags into the trunk of the car, so they were able to keep the different beaches separate. Vickie also dated the bags so that they would not only know where, but when they found them.

Vickie called Jeannie's mom on Sunday morning. They were getting ready for church, and Maggie was going with them. She had borrowed some clothes from Jeannie. Vickie let Susan Henderson know that she and Nick would bring dinner home that evening and that Maggie should be home about 5:00 PM.

As they went through Newport, they stopped at the large Wal-Mart, bought some supplies for Nick's painting business, milk, eggs, bacon, and a couple of pizzas that Vickie would bake when they got home.

Nick pulled Maggie out onto the back deck to show her his sand dollar find. Maggie was stunned at the number of shells that he had and the fact that he had figured out how to add them up and keep track of his debits and credits. She gave him a big hug after praising him for his efforts over the weekend and went inside to talk to her mother.

"Mom, that is amazing what Nick has done. He actually counted all of his sand dollars. I am very impressed," Maggie announced.

"I decided if we were going to do this, I would make a teaching weekend out of it, and he seemed to understand. I am not sure how long he will remember all of it, but at least he grasped the concept this time," Vickie announced. "How was your weekend, honey?"

"Good! We studied for the math test. It is going to be a really hard one, and I need to get a good grade on it to get into the college I want to go to," Maggie explained.

"Where are you planning on going?" Vickie asked with some fear in her voice. She didn't want her to go to a school back east. That was too far away from home.

"I would like to go to Stanford if I can get some scholarships. I know it is one of the more expensive schools around, but it is one of the best for math majors. I know it is very expensive, Mom, and I will apply for all of the scholarships I am eligible for, and I will work in the summers and on weekends and holidays, but that is really where I want to go," Maggie announced in a rush of words.

Vickie was so proud of her daughter at that moment and said, "Don't worry about the cost. Daddy and I had planned a long time ago for our kids' education, and we have a substantial amount set aside for your education. Obviously, Nick will not require the same amount as you do, but we have money set aside for him also. Any scholarships that you can get will be to your advantage, and if you want to work in the summers, that is great, but you don't have to work on weekends or on holidays. Those should be your times for study and for fun," Vickie explained.

While Nick had his mouth full of pizza, he asked Maggie what movie she went to see with Jeannie. "We didn't go to the movie theater. We stayed home and watched a movie on TV. It was one that Mr. Henderson wanted to see again called 'To Kill a Mockingbird' with some actor named Gregory Peck. It was pretty good," Maggie proclaimed.

"What was it about, and why would someone kill the bird?" Nick asked.

"Nick, I'm not sure you would understand, but it was about a lawyer defending a black man who was accused of attacking a white girl," she explained.

"Uck! That sounds boring. If it is not Superman, Batman, or Spiderman, I am not interested!" Nick announced firmly.

Both Maggie and Vickie laughed at him, got up to clean the kitchen while Nick went out to admire his sand dollars again.

Vickie cleaned the glass float and found a bowl to put it in until she could get a stand for it. She placed it on the fireplace mantle and thought it looked very nice there. Maggie was impressed that they had found it. She looked for one every time she went out with Nick to look for sand dollars but had never found one.

Nick took all of his sand dollars to his studio and placed them in neat rows on the shelves. He took scissors and cut out the names of the beaches from the plastic bags and taped them to the shelves below the piles of sand dollars. Then he ran inside and excitedly asked his mom and sister to come see what he had done. Vickie was impressed with the fact that Nick had remembered to keep them separate.

"Mom, Mrs. Carpenter has a board on the wall at school where she puts things on it with funny-looking pins. I need one of those," Nick announced when he was getting ready for bed.

"Do you mean a bulletin board?" she asked.

"I guess so. I think that's what she called it," Nick answered.

"Okay, we can get you a bulletin board. What are you going to put on it?" Vickie asked.

"Just lists and things. Maggie has taken some pictures of my finished sand dollars, and I would like to put some of them up," Nick explained.

A couple of months after Dan died, Vickie had purchased a new sewing machine and serger, thinking that she would start doing some sewing for other people, but she had not even removed the machines from the boxes. Towards the end of May, she realized that the kids would be out of school soon and she would need something else to do to keep herself occupied. Maggie was taking driver's training this semester at school and would be getting her driver's license soon, and Nick would be busy with his sand dollar business all summer. What was she going to do? And where would she put the machines? She had thought about adding another room onto the house off of her bedroom and making it into a sewing room. She had seen pictures in magazines of beautiful rooms where there were shelves and cupboards for all of the supplies and large tables for cutting out patterns. That was really a dream, but she decided to consult Edward Parker, the manager of the garden and feed store, to see if he knew anyone who could give her a bid on a project like that.

After consulting Ed Parker and getting bids from two different builders, and discussing the additional outlay of money with Isaac Steinberg, she decided to go ahead with the project. She wanted a room for her sewing that she could close off when needed and not have everything all over the dining room table.

Vickie chose the firm of Morgan Construction out of Newport for the job. Spencer Morgan gave her a fair bid with a reasonable finish date. He had an architect that he worked with who drew up a set of plans that mirrored exactly what she wanted in a sewing room and blended in with the outside look of the house very well.

Spencer Morgan had owned his business for 24 years. He was 48 years old, a widower with one son. His son was 17 years old and a senior at Newport High School. He was a top athlete, playing on the school's basketball team, and carried a 3.5 or better grade point average. Spencer had converted his garage into an office and built an additional two-car carport alongside the garage. His wife, Amy, had died of cancer when Todd was 14 years old, and Spencer felt it was necessary to be at home for his son. He had a thriving business, doing remodels and additions to private homes. He was always busy, and Todd was his only employee. He worked only on holidays and summers. Spencer had men he could call on to help with some of the heavy work, but most of the time, he worked by himself.

When Vickie Roberts called about an addition to her home in Florence, he was glad for the job. He was only about three days from finishing his current job and wasn't looking forward to having nothing to do. Business had slowed down a little in the last couple of months, and he didn't like being idle. This job would fill in the time from now until Todd's graduation in June. Todd was headed to the University of Oregon in September, and Spencer was not looking forward to having him gone, even if he was at the closest college around. At least he would be able to work with him over the summer.

# CHAPTER 17

Nicholas had a birthday coming up soon. Vickie had asked him what he wanted to do for his birthday, but Nick had not responded favorably. He just told her anything would do. This would be the first birthday without his father, and he wasn't looking forward to it. Vickie talked to Maggie about it, and they finally decided to give Nick a surprise birthday party.

The party was planned for a Saturday afternoon. Vickie arranged to have pizza delivered and ordered a birthday cake from the local bakery, decorating it with sand dollars made of icing. She invited Nick's friends from school and Sunday School and really hoped that Nick would be surprised and happy. Ever since their trip up the coast to look for sand dollars, he had been in his studio most of the time working on them. He had built up quite an inventory by now. They were selling well at George Barnes' IGA grocery, and George thought that they would sell even better when the tourist season began in earnest in June.

Somehow, the party remained a surprise for Nick, and he was excited about having all of his friends there. He was anxious to show them his studio and all of the sand dollars that he was painting. After stuffing themselves with pizza and birthday cake and watching Nick open presents, everyone went home, and Maggie and Vickie cleaned up the mess. Nick went back out to his studio to work on his painting some more.

When Maggie went out to get him to come in at bedtime, she found him sitting on his high stool with his elbows on his table and his head in his hands. He had been crying.

"Sweetheart, what is the matter?" she asked him with concern.

"I thought for sure that Dad would come home for my birthday. Mom, I don't think I did anything wrong to make him mad at me," Nick cried. "I really thought he would be here. I want to show him my sand dollars," Nick cried again.

"Oh, Nicholas!" Vickie cried with him. "I am so sorry you are sad on your birthday. I am not sure how to explain to you that your dad will not be coming home. If he could, he would be here, but he died, Nick. He can't come home. I am sure he would love to be here on your birthday, but he can't. Come in to bed now. You can finish up in here tomorrow after church."

On Monday morning, after Maggie and Nick left for school, Vickie called the child psychologist that Doc Jansen had recommended. Her office was in Newport, but by this time, Vickie was willing to go just about anywhere to get help for Nicholas. She had reached her limit and did not know where to go from here. Dr. Naomi Caravelle gave her an appointment the next day at 10:00 in the morning. It was a perfect time for Vickie. She would be able to get back home before the kids got home from school. On Wednesday morning, Spencer Morgan was to come to start the work on her sewing room addition, and she absolutely had to be there. She didn't want to delay that project at all.

Nick was very quiet when he got home from school. Maggie indicated to her mother that he was in a real funk and to be careful. He snapped at her on the way home and was pretty angry about something.

He absolutely refused to do his homework and tried to go out to his studio to paint. Vickie told him that he could not go out until his homework was finished.

"You know the rules, Nicholas. No homework – no painting. If you refuse to do your homework, you will not be allowed to go to your studio," Vickie announced. "Your studio is locked until I see that your homework has been finished."

Nick started screaming at his mother that she couldn't do that to him, that was his studio, and that she had no right to lock him out of it. Maggie came out of her room when she heard Nick screaming. She took one look at him and went over and slapped him in the face. He was startled by her action and started to hit her, but she grabbed hold of his arms with one hand and slapped him again. Nick sputtered a couple of times, then just collapsed on the floor in tears.

Maggie dropped down beside him and took him in her arms and held him while he cried. "I want my dad," was all he could say. "I want my dad."

Vickie stood there in the kitchen, stunned at what had just occurred between her children. How did Maggie know what to do to get him to stop his tantrum? Vickie's heart was breaking for her son. She couldn't imagine what he had been going through all of this time, except that she had been going through her own version of hell since Dan's death.

Maggie finally led Nick back into his bedroom and onto his bed. "Sleep for a while, Nicky, then you will feel better."

"Call me Nick or Nicholas, please, Maggie," Nick said as he started to fall asleep. Maggie kissed him on the forehead and slowly left his bedroom.

"What just happened, Maggie?" Vickie asked in wonder.

"I have been reading some books about taking care of special needs kids. This sounds horrible, Mom, but I figured that with Dad gone, if something happened to you, I would be responsible for taking care of Nick. I wanted to know what to do and how to raise him properly. This was one suggestion on how to pull him out of a tantrum," Maggie explained her actions.

"Well, it worked. I don't know if he will ever talk to me again, but it worked. Is he sleeping now?" she asked her daughter.

"Yeah. He laid down on his very messy bed, and I covered him with his blanket."

"Thanks, Mags! I appreciate your stepping in and defusing the situation. I am kind of at my wits' end. I have an appointment tomorrow morning in Newport with a child psychologist to talk about Nick. I need help, and so does he. Maybe this is the way to go," she explained. "I will pull him out of school for appointments if I have to. I will let you know what the schedule will be. Thanks again, honey. You saved the day," Vickie said, very grateful for such a smart daughter.

Dr. Naomi Caravelle was a woman of about 60 years old. She had been a partner in a large firm in Portland before branching out on her own when she and her husband moved to Newport. She and her husband had since divorced, he moving to the East Coast and she remaining in Newport to start her own practice.

Vickie found her very knowledgeable and very willing to work her schedule around Nick's school hours. Three days a week, Vickie would pull him out of school a half hour early to make the drive to Newport. Dr. Caravelle admitted that she had not done a lot of work with special needs children and the subject of the death of a parent, but she was willing and eager to work with Nick. She did explain to Vickie that there would be some sessions with the both of them, but most of them would be with Nick alone. And, there might be times when she would want Maggie in on the appointments.

Vickie drove home, very relieved that she would be getting help with Nick. She drove to the school to let the office know what she would be doing Monday, Wednesday, and Friday, and to let Mrs. Carpenter in on her plans. She drove home after that to find Nick in his studio and Maggie in her room studying.

"He would not listen to me at all. He said that I am not the boss of him and I couldn't tell him what to do. He is very angry with you for not being here when he got home, so watch out when you go out there," Maggie explained to her mother.

"Thanks, honey. Sorry to have to put you in this position. I have made a series of appointments with a child psychologist in Newport. I will be taking him out of school a half hour early on Monday, Wednesday, and Friday, so we won't be home on those days when you get home from school. I hope that is all right," Vickie asked.

"He needs the help, Mom. I will be fine," Maggie answered.

Vickie went out to the studio then to face her angry child. Nick did not hear her come into the studio, and when she put her arm on his shoulder, he spun around and almost hit her. He had venom in his eyes.

"Where were you?" he yelled at her. "My dad would never have left me here alone."

Vickie purposefully kept her voice low and steady and said, "First of all, you were not alone. Your sister was here with you. I was at a doctor's appointment in Newport. I told you this morning before you left for school that I might not be here when you got home, but to go ahead and do your homework before you came out here. May I see your homework, please?" Vickie asked.

"I didn't do it, and I am not going to do any more homework. I don't like homework," Nick announced.

"In the house, Nicholas!" Vickie ordered her son.

"No! I am not done here yet," Nick stated.

Vickie took his arm, got him off of his stool, and led him towards the door. "In the house, Nicholas!" she said again. He tried to yank free of her grasp, but she held on and led him towards the door. As they left, Vickie locked the door.

"I will just break the window and get in anyway," Nick cried.

"You do, and I will have everything packed away and have the shed taken out of the yard. Don't think I don't mean it, Nicholas, because I do," Vickie announced as she led him back into the house.

Nick spent the rest of the evening in his room—he did not come out to eat dinner or say good night. Vickie looked in on him several times to make sure he was okay, but he was sleeping every time, so she didn't disturb him.

After a restless night's sleep, Vickie got up early to fix her kids a nice breakfast before school. Maggie was up and in the kitchen when Nick came in. He handed his mother a crumpled piece of paper without saying anything to her. It was his homework assignment, very messy and crumpled up, and with every math problem incorrect, but at least he had done it.

"Thank you, Nick," Vickie said very gently and handed the paper back to him. "You may turn this in to Mrs. Carpenter this morning."

Nick very sheepishly took the paper back and sat down to eat his breakfast. He had not eaten any supper the night before and devoured four slices of French toast and two glasses of orange juice before he got up, gathered up his backpack, and walked out the door behind his sister.

"Have a good day, Nick," called his mother after him, but he just walked away without saying a word.

As Maggie was walking along with Nick on their way to school, she said, "Nick, that was really a mean thing to do to Mom. You didn't even say goodbye to her."

"Well, she has been mean to me, so why should I be nice to her?" Nick asked.

"Mom has not been mean to you, Nick. She is just trying to teach you to obey the rules. You know there is no painting until homework is done. Do you know that if she let you quit school now, she could go to jail?" Maggie tried to explain to Nick. "It is against the law for a young person not to go to school before they turn 18 years old. It is called truancy. Do you want Mom to go to jail?"

"No, but she shouldn't lock me out of my own studio. I want to paint," Nick complained.

"I know you want to paint, Nick, and you do a great job of it, but all you have to do is finish your homework and show it to Mom, and then she will let you paint," Maggie tried to explain to him. "Mom is trying real hard to be a good mother to us. She misses Dad too, you know."

"I don't think she does. I think she is the one who won't let him come home to see us," Nick stated firmly.

Maggie stopped walking and stood there with a shocked look on her face. Then she said, "Nicholas, that is ridiculous! Dad is dead. He died of a heart attack last October. Mom has told you that many times. Please don't ever say that to her. She would be so hurt if she knew you said that."

"I can't help what I think!" Nick mumbled as he headed up the walk to his school. Maggie crossed the street to the high school, very upset with her brother.

Vickie had scheduled her day so that she could leave to pick up Nick early from school for the drive to Newport to visit Dr. Caravelle. She wasn't sure what Nick's reaction would be to leaving school early and going to the doctor, but she would just have to deal with him.

# CHAPTER 18

aomi Caravelle had a doctorate in child psychology from Harvard. She had received her bachelor's and master's degrees from the University of Oregon in Eugene. She was well thought of in the field and had published several papers on dealing with children and the death of a parent, but had not had a lot of experience dealing with special needs children and the death of a parent.

In preparation for her appointment with Vickie Roberts and her son Nicholas, she had researched as much information as she could on the subject. She had purposefully scheduled herself a half hour of downtime before they arrived so she could put her feet up and rest a bit.

Nick was very surprised when he was called to the office before school was out on Monday and even more surprised to see his mom there waiting for him. Mrs. Carpenter had told him to take his coat and papers with him and that she would see him the next day. He was sure he was in a lot of trouble for the way he treated his mom that morning. He had felt kind of bad about it all day and was going to apologize to her after he got home.

Vickie was waiting in the office for Nick. She really felt sorry for him when she saw him. He was obviously scared. It had been a very rare occasion when she had pulled him out of school early.

"Hi," Vickie said. "We have a doctor's appointment in Newport this afternoon, and we have to leave before school's out to get there on time."

"I'm not sick. Why do I need to go to a doctor?" Nick asked, looking at his mother with fear in his eyes.

"She is a different kind of doctor," Vickie explained as they got into the car. "She is going to talk to us and listen to how we answer her questions. Sometimes, she will talk to you by yourself, without me there. That way you can tell her things that you don't want to tell me. And sometimes, she is going to let you play some games. Maybe she will even ask you to paint something for her."

Nick was quiet for a while and then said, "She sounds like a weird doctor, Mom!"

Nick was fairly quiet the rest of the way into Newport. Vickie knew he was trying to process what she had told him about the new doctor.

Dr. Caravelle asked both Vickie and Nick some basic questions about themselves and their life in Florence. She asked Nick about his sand dollars.

"Why don't you bring some the next time you come? I might want to buy some of them from you. I have a lot of friends that live in areas where they don't have sand dollars. They would make a very nice gift for me to send to them," the doctor said to him.

Nick's whole face lit up at her request. "How many do you want me to bring?" he asked with amazement.

"Oh, I think six would be good," the doctor answered.

After they had been in her office talking for an hour, Dr. Caravelle said that their time was up for that day, but she was really looking forward to seeing them on Wednesday and seeing the sand dollars that Nick would bring.

"Mrs. Roberts, I think I would like to talk to Nick by himself on Wednesday, if you don't mind. All of this sand dollar talk might get a little boring for you," the doctor said.

"I will bring a good book to read while you and my son discuss his business. Thank you, doctor," Vickie said. "We will see you on Wednesday."

Nick was quiet for a while, then said, "She was nice, Mom. She wants to buy some of my sand dollars. Will you unlock my studio so I can choose the ones I want to take?"

"Sure, I will. That is quite an honor, Nick. You do good work, and when people want to see your work, that is a compliment to you and the work," Vickie explained.

"When do we go back to see her?" Nick questioned.

"On Wednesday. That is the day after tomorrow. I will pick you up early from school again," Vickie explained to her son.

"She's a nice lady, Mom. She is fun to talk to, especially when she talks about my sand dollars. Hey, Mom, when I sell the sand dollars to her, do I have to give Mr. Barnes part of the money?" Nick asked his mom.

"No, you don't. If you sell them yourself, you get to keep the whole amount. That will really help build your bank account up. When we get home, we can figure out how much that will be," Vickie told Nick.

"Okay. I like the idea of keeping all of the money. I need to go to the beach and find more, though. Maybe we could go on a trip again to hunt for them. We did pretty good last time," Nick suggested to his mom.

"Honey, we are not going to be able to go away for a while. A man is coming to the house tomorrow to start adding another room onto the house," Vickie tried to explain to Nick.

"Why do we need another room?" he asked.

"I want a sewing room. You know how you have your studio to paint in. I want a sewing room to sew in. I want to be able to set my new sewing machine and serger up on tables and leave them there. I don't want to have to put everything away so that we can eat on the table," Vickie explained.

"Where are you going to make this room, Mom?" Nick inquired.

"It will be right off of my bedroom. There will be a door from my bedroom into the sewing room. I will have nice large windows so that I can have plenty of light. I want to start sewing for other people as well as Maggie. I can earn some extra money that way," Vickie almost said to herself. She was dreaming about how the room would look.

"Hey, Mom! Maybe we could have our businesses together. That would be neat. I think I will tell my new doctor about it," Nick said enthusiastically.

When Vickie and Nick walked into the kitchen, Maggie was busy putting together a tuna and noodle casserole for their supper. She had made a tossed salad and opened a package of frozen carrots to go with the meal.

"Wow!" said Vickie. "And what did we do to deserve this wonderful surprise?"

"You are just a good mom. Nick, you have time to go do your homework before this casserole is done. Then I thought that if it is okay with Mom, you and I would go down to the beach and look for shells. There was a higher than normal tide today, and maybe there will be some good sand dollars that were pushed up," Maggie announced.

"Can we, Mom?" Nick begged.

"Sure, if your homework is finished," Vickie emphasized.

"I will go do it now," Nick announced as he rushed off to his room.

"Thanks, Maggie! That was a change. He has been grumbling lately about doing his homework, but the thought of going to the beach spurred him on. I have to move some stuff around in my bedroom in order for Mr. Morgan to start work on the new room tomorrow morning. I am really excited about the room I will have, especially the storage space. All of my boxes of different materials and supplies will be able to come out of the garage and into a clean, dry place," Vickie explained to Maggie.

"I wonder if his son is going to help him," Maggie mused.

"I didn't know he had a son," Vickie said.

"Yeah. His name is Todd. He is a senior this year. I heard he is going to Oregon next year," Maggie said as she headed off to her room to do her homework.

Vickie looked at her daughter and thought that she was going to have to keep an eagle eye on her, or she would be out there all of the time if Todd did come with his dad. Maggie was a very striking girl and seemed to attract a lot of attention from the boys. Vickie had not allowed her to go out on dates yet. She felt she was too young, but she knew the day would come soon. In two years, she would be going away to school. It was something that Vickie did not want to think about. The idea of Dan not being here to see his little girl grow up was sometimes more than she could bear.

Oh well, back to work. Enough thinking, more doing!

Spencer Morgan arrived early Tuesday morning, ready to get busy on his new construction project. He liked the idea of adding the room onto the Roberts house. He thought that it would make the house look more symmetrical and would also enhance the value of the house should Mrs. Roberts want to sell at some time. Todd would come over after school to help him set the boards for the foundation to be poured. He would grade the land today and get it ready for the framing. The cement truck was scheduled for Thursday, so he had to get the frame in quickly. Fortunately, the weather forecast was good, and no rain was predicted. School would be out in two weeks, and Todd's graduation was scheduled for the first week in June. Boy, how he missed Marie now. Todd was graduating, and she would not be here to see it. It was going to be hard sending him off to school in September. He had not lived alone for 20 years.

Oh well, enough of these maudlin thoughts. He had work to do. As he rang the doorbell at the Roberts home, a young boy came bounding out of the door and ran smack into him.

"Hello!" Spencer said. "Are you the man of the house?" he said to Nick as Nick looked up at him in wonder and didn't say anything for a minute.

"Mom!" Nick yelled. "There is a man out here who wants to know if I am the man of the house. Am I?"

Spencer laughed at that comment and was still laughing when Vickie came to the door with a big smile on her face. Just then, a very pretty girl came to the door.

"Hello, Mr. Morgan. I am Maggie Roberts," she introduced herself. "Come on, Nick, we have to get to school."

"Well, am I the man of the house?" he asked, looking at the tall man standing on his front porch.

"Yes, Nick. You are the man of the house," his mother answered.

"But when Dad comes back, then he will be again. Right, Mom?" Nick stated, still believing that his dad would come back.

"Off to school with you!" Vickie said emphatically.

"Sorry about that, Mr. Morgan. Nicholas is always full of questions. Please come in. Would you like a cup of coffee?" Vickie asked.

"That would be nice. Just black, please, and please call me Spence. Mr. Morgan was my father, and is what my son's friends call me. To my peers, I am Spence or Spencer," he said.

"And I am Vickie. That young man that just left is my son, Nick, and the young lady is my daughter, Maggie. Maggie walks Nick to school every day. He is in the special ed classes at the elementary school and has been teased and bullied by some of the older high school boys. When Maggie is with him, they do not bother him. Unfortunately, there is not much I can do about it. I have talked to the administration at the high school, but they have no inclination to reprimand the bullies at this time. So as long as Maggie is with him, he is okay," Vickie explained.

"I'm sorry to hear that. I was bullied when I was young. I had buck teeth and then braces. It was a horrible feeling to be bullied for something you could not prevent. My parents spent a fortune on my teeth in order for me to have a normal smile, but the process was torture both in the pain of mouth and of spirit," explained Spencer.

"Well, on to happier subjects. What is your process for starting this project?" Vickie asked.

"I will stake out the area and grade it to get ready to put the frames up for the foundation to be poured. I have the cement truck scheduled for Thursday, so I will grade today and tomorrow morning and then get the frames up tomorrow afternoon and evening. My son Todd will come after school and work with me. He is becoming an accomplished carpenter. He has worked for me since he was 14. Unfortunately, I am going to lose him after the summer is over. He goes off to college in the fall," Spencer explained the process of getting the land ready for the construction.

"Well, I will let you get to it. If you need anything, just let me know," Vickie said as she let Spencer out the front door and went into the kitchen to have another cup of coffee and pay some bills. Vickie was doing fairly well financially. She was receiving a small income each month from her investments along with Dan's Social Security survivors benefits and benefits for the kids. She was also receiving the monthly payment from Harry Young at the lumber yard. Because she had no mortgage to pay, she was in pretty good shape financially. She hoped that she would also make some extra money from sewing. She kind of thought that she might put that aside to help finance a nice vacation with the kids next summer. She really wanted to take them to Disneyland. Dan had always talked about going, but they had not gotten around to it.

As Vickie was sitting and paying her bills, she saw the property tax bill for the cabin in the mountains. They had only been there once since Dan died, and it was not a pleasant experience being there without him. She wondered if she should sell the place. She didn't really want to get rid of it, but it was just sitting there empty. She knew that Nick would be very upset if she sold it. Maybe she should make a trip up there sometime during a day when the kids were in school. She needed to make a decision one way or the other, but didn't want to do it until she had been there again.

# CHAPTER 19

---◆•◆•◆•◆---

Spencer worked with the grader all day on Tuesday and made good headway on leveling the ground to set the framing for the concrete foundation. When Nick and Maggie got home from school, Nick was right outside watching Spencer, fascinated by what he was doing to his yard. Bushes were taken out along the side of the house and put into large containers to be replanted when the room was completed.

"Nicholas, homework!" Vickie reminded her son.

"But Mom! I want to watch what he is doing to the yard," Nick begged.

"Nicholas, you know the rules. Inside, now!" Vickie demanded. "Do you have all of your sand dollars ready to take to Dr. Caravelle tomorrow?"

"Yes," Nick answered, dejected that he had to leave the excitement of the work in the yard.

"Good. Let's put them in the car as soon as you finish your homework so we won't forget them tomorrow. I will pick you up from school early so we can get to our appointment on time," Vickie explained.

On the way to the doctor Wednesday afternoon, Nick asked his mom about talking to the doctor by himself. "What am I going to say to her, Mom?"

"I don't know, Nick. She will probably ask you some questions. Just answer them as best you can. I will be in the waiting room, but you will do fine."

When his time with Dr. Caravelle was up, Nick came bounding out of her office waving $30.00 in his hand. "Look, Mom!" he hollered. "She bought all six of my sand dollars. I need to go to the bank right now."

Both Vickie and the doctor were laughing. "That is very nice, Nick. Did you thank her?"

"Thanks," Nick turned around and said to the doctor. "Mom, we have to go to the bank now."

"The bank will be closed by the time we get home, but we will put your money in a safe place tonight, and we can go tomorrow after school," Vickie explained.

"On Friday, I will want to talk to all three of you. Can you bring your daughter in then?"

"Yes. We will see you then," Vickie said as she was ushering Nick out of the office.

Nick was quiet on the way home. He kept looking at the $30.00 he had in his hand. "This is a lot of money, isn't it, Mom?" Nick said.

"Yes, it is. You are very lucky, Nick," Vickie answered.

"Where am I going to put my money until you can take me to the bank tomorrow?" Nick asked.

"How about if I get you an envelope and you can put it in there? If you want, I can put it in my purse, and I can pick you and Maggie up at school tomorrow and go directly to the bank," Vickie suggested.

"That sounds like a good idea, Mom!" Nick stated. "Don't forget my bank book. I need that for the man at the bank to put down the amount I am giving him. He keeps track of the total for me. I have quite a bit of money now, don't I, Mom?"

"Yes, you do!" Vickie assured him.

When Vickie and Nick drove into the driveway, they noticed that Spencer was still working on the side yard. His son, Todd, was working with him on putting the grading machine back on its trailer. Vickie also noticed that Maggie was standing on the far side of the lawn watching what was going on. She suspected that Maggie was watching Todd more than the procedure of getting the machine onto the trailer.

As Nick was headed over to watch the loading process, Vickie called to him to come in and do his homework before anything else. She also called Maggie into the house to let her know about Friday's visit to the doctor.

"Dr. Caravelle is going to want to see all three of us on Friday, so I will pick you up early from school also. I think she is going to talk about your dad, and she wants both of us there when she speaks with Nicholas," Vickie explained.

"Darn! I wanted to invite Jeannie over after school on Friday. She wants to meet Todd," Maggie announced.

"You leave Todd alone. He is here to work, not to socialize with you or your friends," Vickie admonished her daughter.

"Yes, Mother," Maggie answered back to her mom.

Both Spencer and Todd left a few minutes later, Spencer letting Vickie know that he would get the rest of the framing done the next day and the cement truck would be there in the afternoon to pour the foundation. He explained to Vickie that the cement would dry until Monday, then they would take the framing off and start construction on the walls.

"Dad, Maggie Roberts was telling me about her brother Nick. She said that she has to walk him to and from school so that he won't be bullied. If he is by himself, some of the older boys bully and tease him so much that he is in tears. That's not right. No one should have to go through that," Todd explained to his dad.

"You're right. No one should. It is a shame about Nick because he is really a good kid. Do you know that he paints the sand dollars that George sells at the grocery store?" Spence asked.

"Yeah! Maggie was telling me about collecting them and how he cleans them and paints them. She says he is pretty good, and Mr. Barnes sells quite a few of them to tourists. I don't think some of those bullies know that Nick is the one painting them," Todd mused.

"Todd, please don't get involved with Maggie Roberts. She is only 15 years old, and you are 18. That could mean trouble if you get too involved with her," Spence warned.

"Don't worry, Dad. Patty is enough to keep me busy. I don't know how much longer I will be going out with her. She wants more than I am ready to give. She doesn't think I should go away to school, that I should stay here and work with you and make it my career, but I am not interested in Maggie or any other girl now. I will be leaving in the fall. I think I know some of the guys who are bullying Nick. I am going to talk to them. What do you think?"

"That's a good idea if you think you can make a difference, but be sure that you have your facts straight before you get in too deep," Spencer commented.

"Thanks, Dad. I will!" Todd answered.

The next day at lunch, Todd sat down with some of the guys who had been bullying Nick Roberts. Todd had said "Hi" to Maggie as he walked into the lunchroom, and when he sat down, one of the other fellows said, "Hey, Morgan, isn't that the sister of the retard from the special ed class in the other school? She's pretty fine-looking. You getting anything from her?"

"Her name is Maggie Roberts, and her brother's name is Nick Roberts, and yes, she is a very nice-looking girl, and no, I am not going out with her. She is a sophomore. My dad and I are putting an addition onto her house. And I am offended by you calling her brother a retard. He does have some learning difficulties and is in a special ed class, but did you know that Nick Roberts is the one who paints the sand dollars that Mr. Barnes sells in the grocery? He is a very talented painter," Todd explained. "Why do you bully him?"

"It's fun to see him cry," one of the other boys said.

"You have red hair. What would you do if you were 10 years old and I teased you about your red hair? Bruce, you are left-handed. What if I teased you about being left-handed? Greg, you are short. What if I teased you about being short? None of you can help being what you are. You were born that way. Well, Nick can't help being the way he is, but at least he is trying to improve. He is painting beautiful sand dollars, and he is selling them. That is more than I can say for any of you," Todd emphasized as he got up from the table and moved to another table to sit beside Patty, who had been giving him dirty looks for not sitting beside her as soon as he walked into the lunchroom.

Graduation was only two weeks away. Todd was named valedictorian of his graduating class and was busy working on his speech. He wanted to make it different from other valedictorian speeches in the past. He had made a monumental decision in the past few weeks. He was going to change his major from business administration to special education. He had been getting to know Nick Roberts and had seen what a need there was for good, qualified people to teach special needs students. He was almost possessed about the need to help someone like Nick reach his full potential.

Spencer was very surprised at Todd's decision. He had always assumed that with a degree in business, he would take over the construction business and make it grow into a successful enterprise. Not that it wasn't successful now, but Spence had always hoped that it would be large enough to bid on big construction projects. He didn't have the resources either in money or manpower to do that now.

But he was proud of Todd for the decision that he made. God knew that good teachers were needed in our school systems.

Maggie was singing in the school choir, and they were performing at graduation, so Vickie and Nick had tickets to the ceremony as well. Graduation was one of the highlights of the school year in Florence, Oregon, and it seemed that the whole town was out for the ceremony. This year, it was held in the newly repaired civic stadium. The stadium was damaged during the tsunami last summer, and graduation was the first big event being held there.

Nick was excited about seeing his new friend Todd get up and give a speech. He had never known anyone who spoke in front of such a large crowd before. Todd gave a good speech about his desire to teach special education and the need for good teachers. He also mentioned how much he had enjoyed his participation in the extracurricular activities at school and ended with saying, "I want to give a special thanks to my good friend Nick Roberts. He is sitting out in this audience today. Nick has taught me about living life to the fullest and enjoying what you do. If you didn't know, Nick is the one who paints the sand dollars that Mr. Barnes sells at the IGA. Nick is a very talented painter and will go far in his career. Nick is enrolled in the special education classes at the elementary school and has learned to use his special talents to the fullest. Keep learning, Nick! I love you!"

Nick, Vickie, and Maggie, along with Todd's dad, Spencer, were awestruck at Todd's speech. All three of the Roberts were in tears. The graduating class stood up together and gave him a standing ovation, along with most of the audience.

"Nick, because of what Todd said about your sand dollars, you will have to get busy and paint some more. Mr. Barnes might need to restock. With school out in a week, there will be a lot more visitors to the beach, and they will want something to take home. Your sand dollars would be the perfect thing," Vickie explained.

"Maybe we could go to the beach and see if we can find some more, Mom," Nick responded to his mom.

"Let's do that on Saturday morning. You will have to get up very early. There will probably be a lot of people out that day, and we want to get an early start," Vickie said. "Maggie, do you want to come along?"

"Sure. I would like to. Can we go up the beach to Yachats or Waldport? We might have better luck up there. Because I have my driver's permit now, maybe I could drive?" Maggie asked with a hopeful look in her eyes.

"I think that can be arranged. It would be a good time for you to practice," Vickie answered.

"Thanks, Mom!" Maggie said as she bounded off to her room to change her clothes.

# CHAPTER 20

ickie informed Spencer Morgan that they would be leaving very early on Saturday morning. He had let Vickie know that he and Todd would be working six days a week to get her room finished as soon as possible. Vickie trusted Spencer enough to give him a key to the house so that he could use the bathroom and the kitchen if needed for his lunch when she wasn't there.

Maggie was up very early on Saturday morning and was already sitting in the driver's seat of the car by the time Vickie and Nicholas came out to the garage.

As they drove up the coast, Nick talked constantly about Maggie's driving. "Maggie, you are going too slow! Maggie, you are going too fast! Maggie, you are getting too close to the edge of the road!" — and on and on he went.

"Nicholas, you are getting on my nerves. Please be quiet!" Maggie said.

"Well, I don't like the way you drive. I want Mom to drive," Nick stated emphatically.

"How am I going to learn if I don't drive? Just be quiet for a change, Nick," Maggie said.

"Maggie, please don't talk to your brother that way. He is only expressing his concerns. Maybe it would be better if just you and I went out instead of taking Nick with us. You might feel better about driving, and your nerves wouldn't get so frayed," Vickie told her.

"Okay. That's a good idea. I will pull off onto the next turnoff and you can drive," Maggie stated with relief. "It isn't as much fun with him in the back seat anyway."

They drove up to Yachats Beach and found several good sand dollars very near the water line. Some of them still had the fuzz on them. They also found several on the beach at Waldport.

They drove on up to Newport and had breakfast at a new place that had just opened up. Then Vickie suggested that they visit some of the gift shops in town to see what they were selling in the way of souvenirs. She thought that maybe Nick could try some other types of shells to be painted. She wanted him to see what was available and to make his own decision if he wanted to do something else along with the sand dollars.

Nick had loved going to Todd's graduation ceremony and felt very good when Todd mentioned him in his speech, but other than that bright spot, he had been very quiet and somewhat tense since Friday's meeting with Dr. Caravelle. She talked to all three of them about Dan and how his death had affected them. Vickie and Maggie were very clear about their feelings and were able to express them to the doctor, but Nick became very argumentative.

"My dad is away. Mom says he is never coming back, but I don't believe her. He would not leave me. He will come back. Sometimes I think that my mom does not want him to come back. She acts like she rules the house now and Dad doesn't count," Nick explained to the doctor. He had started to cry when he was talking to her, and Vickie started to put her arm around him to comfort him, but the doctor stopped her.

"Let him work it out himself," she said. "He needs to come to terms with his grief. Your time is about up, and I have another patient who will be here shortly, but I think that on Monday, I will speak to Nick alone. We have some things to work through."

"Thank you, Doctor. See you on Monday," Vickie said as she herded her kids out the door and toward their car. "How about some dinner here in Newport? We could have some fish and chips if you want," Vickie suggested.

"No! I just want to go home and paint. I have some sand dollars to finish for Mr. Barnes," Nick announced in a very surly voice.

"Do you have any homework, Nick?" Vickie asked very gently. She didn't want to rile him up while she was driving.

"No. Mrs. Carpenter didn't give us any, so I can go home and start painting," Nick said with determination in his voice now.

"You will have to change your clothes and eat dinner when I get it fixed," she said.

"Okay, let's eat here, and then I can get busy right away at home. Dad would let me paint whenever I wanted to. He wouldn't make me do other things," Nick mumbled.

Maggie reached over and put her hand on Vickie's shoulder to comfort her. Vickie had tears running down her face, but she wiped them away and didn't say anything to Nick regarding his comment about Dan.

When they got home, they noticed that two of the walls of the addition were up. Nick ran over to look at the progress. He was sorry that he missed watching the walls go up.

"They will probably put the other two up tomorrow. If you stay out of their way, you can probably watch that. After the walls go up, they will cut the opening for the door to my bedroom and then put the roof on. It is exciting to watch the progress," Vickie said as she sidled over to Nick and put her arm around his shoulders.

"Yeah, it's exciting, but it was more exciting when you had my studio put in. That was cool how they put it together," Nick said.

After he changed his clothes, he went directly to his studio. Maggie told him to come in for dinner when it was ready, but Nick said that he wasn't hungry and wanted to keep painting.

The next day, Spencer and Todd did put up the other two sides of the room. Nick watched in fascination, as did Vickie and Maggie. They stood on the far end of the lawn so as not to get in the way. Spencer had one other friend of Todd's there helping them. It took three strong men to lift the walls and anchor them down. After that was done, Spencer informed her that it was time to cut the doorway out from her bedroom.

Vickie was surprised that the roof would not be put on first.

"We need to make sure that the measurements are correct and that the roof will fit properly over the door. It would not be a good idea for you to come through the door and have rain dripping on you," Spencer said, grinning at her. "I will come in on Monday and cover everything with plastic. You might want to move out of your room for a couple of nights," he suggested.

"I can bunk in with Maggie. She has an extra bed in her room," Vickie said.

"Mom, I was just talking to Jeannie and telling her about them cutting a door into your room. She asked if I wanted to sleep over at her house for the weekend so that you can use my bed," Maggie explained to her mom.

"That would be okay, and I guess I can walk Nick to school on Monday morning. I will call Susan and thank her. Maybe I will see if Nick wants to drive south on the highway and look for shells. I don't know if he will open up and talk to me, but it's worth a try," Vickie said.

Early Saturday morning, Vickie and Nick headed out for the southern Oregon coast to see what they could find along the beach. They stopped at several of the beaches to search for sand dollars and had some luck in finding good ones. Nick was excited about the size of the sand dollars. He thought they were larger than the ones he had found before. They stopped in Reedsport for breakfast, then headed south again.

"Mom, with all of these sand dollars I am finding, I think I am going to need some more paint. I would like to try some different colors this time. I am getting tired of the ones I have," Nick announced.

"Sure. We can get some more paint for you. I think there is a pretty good craft store in Coos Bay. How about stopping there to look? You might see something else you need too. And I would like to look for some storage boxes and shelves that would work in my sewing room," Vickie added.

"Hey, Mom, you brought a suitcase with you. Are we going to stay in a motel someplace?" Nick asked.

"I think so. It might be too late to drive back home this evening. And I always bring a change of clothes with us when we go to the beaches away from our own. I put in your pajamas, just in case we decided to stay out until tomorrow. It will be an adventure for us," Vickie explained the reason for the suitcase.

"What about Maggie? Won't she be worried about us?" Nick asked.

"She knows we might stay away until tomorrow, and she is at Jeannie's house, so she's okay," Vickie assured her son.

They stopped at almost all of the beaches along the way and drove as far as Brookings, the last city in Oregon before the California border. Vickie found the southern beaches less crowded than the ones north of Florence, and they found a treasure trove of not only sand dollars but other types of shells. They found quite a few large and unbroken scallop shells, and Nick was excited about maybe trying to paint pictures on those.

They stayed the night in Brookings, had fish and chips for dinner, and settled into the motel to watch TV. Vickie tried to get Nick to talk to her about seeing Dr. Caravelle, but he clammed up every time she said something about her and refused to talk. She decided not to push the subject. They were having such a good time, and she didn't want to spoil it.

On the way home on Sunday, Vickie stopped in Reedsport to call Maggie and let her know where they were and that they would be home soon.

"I'll go home soon and be there when you get home, Mom," Maggie said.

"Thanks, sweetie! See you soon," Vickie said and then walked back to the car where Nick was waiting for her.

"Mom, why do you let Maggie be home alone and don't let me be home alone?" Nick asked out of the blue.

"Probably because Maggie is 16 years old and you are only 10. I didn't let Maggie stay home alone when she was 10 years old. I think 10 is a little young to be on your own," Vickie explained. "Why do you ask?"

"I was just thinking. I think about a lot of things, Mom. One of the main things I think about, besides sand dollars, is why Dad never comes home anymore," Nick told her. "I really miss him."

"I've explained to you before, Nick, that your dad got sick and he died. His heart just stopped beating. The doctors tried very hard to get it beating again, but they couldn't do it. Nick, Dad didn't want to die. He really wanted to stay with us, but it just didn't happen. You know, I think God needed him to help him up in heaven. I miss him too, all of the time," Vickie explained. She had tears running down her face as she talked, and she had to pull over to the side of the road to get a tissue to wipe her eyes.

Nick was looking at her when she pulled over but not saying anything. "Do you understand what I have told you, Nick? Dad can't come back in person, but he will always be with you in your heart if you let him."

"Okay, Mom. Can we go home now? I need to clean some of these sand dollars we got," Nick announced. It seemed that the conversation about his dad was finished.

# CHAPTER 21

In Nick's sessions with Dr. Caravelle, it seemed as though he had accepted the fact that his dad was dead. "My mom told me that Dad's heart just stopped beating and none of the doctors could make it beat again. Your heart has to beat in order to stay alive. Did you know that?"

"I had heard that, Nick. What do you think happens to them after their heart stops beating?" the doctor asked very seriously.

"Well, I guess maybe they go up to heaven and work with God. That's what my mom said that my dad probably did," Nick explained. "Mom also said that when I'm 16 like Maggie is now, I will be able to stay at home by myself. That will be fun."

"I'll bet there will be rules that you have to follow, though," Dr. Caravelle said.

"There are always rules that I have to follow!" Nick announced very succinctly.

"Me too, Nick. Me too!" she answered. "On Wednesday, I would like to see both you and your mom. Will that be okay?" the doctor asked.

"Sure. Do you want Maggie here too? She likes to get out of school an hour early," Nick asked.

"Okay. That would be fine with me," Dr. Caravelle said.

Nick waved as he walked out the door of her office and went to his mom to relay all of the information about the next appointment. Nick seemed to accept the fact that his father was dead. He talked about him more than he had before and did not say anything that would make Vickie believe that he thought he would come home soon.

People in town were talking about "Sand Dollars by Nicholas" and were buying them up just about as fast as Nick could get them to George Barnes at the grocery store. He was starting to branch out and use some different colors and different designs. Maggie had found him some bright neon-colored paints, and he loved working with them.

"Mom, I think I need to have a sign to put up where my sand dollars are sold. It should let people know that it is me who is painting them," Nick announced one morning at breakfast. School was out for the summer, so Nick spent more time at the kitchen table in the morning. Maggie was usually still in bed, and it was Nick's alone time with his mom.

"How big of a sign do you want?" Vickie asked.

"Not a real big one. Something that could sit on a table maybe. I want it to say 'Sand Dollars painted by Nick."

"I think that is a very good idea. Do you want to paint it yourself, or do you want someone else to do it for you?" Vickie asked Nick, who was munching on his second bowl of Corn Puffs.

"Probably someone else," Nick said as Corn Puffs fell out of his mouth and back into his bowl.

"Nick, when are you going to learn to eat without food spilling out of your mouth?" Maggie asked as she walked into the room in her nightgown and bathrobe. "That looks gross!"

"Hi, Maggie!" Nick said to his sister. "I am going to have a real sign made with my name on it and everything. I can put it up wherever I sell my sand dollars."

Maggie just looked at Nick and proceeded to get a bowl and pour herself some Corn Puffs.

"Kids, I want to talk to you for a moment," Vickie said to her children.

"We are already talking, Mom," Nick said.

"This is very important, and I need your full attention," Vickie assured them.

"My sand dollars are important too, Mom," Nick said with a hurt look on his face.

"I know they are, Nick, but we have something else to talk about now. We need to make a decision about the cabin in the mountains and what we are going to do with it. We have only been there once since your dad died, and that was only for a few hours," Vickie explained.

"I didn't have any fun when we were there last time. It isn't the same without Dad there," Nick announced.

"I didn't have any fun either," Maggie announced. "It is creepy there without Dad."

"I wanted to ask you if you think we should sell it?" Vickie asked her children.

Both Maggie and Nick looked a little surprised, but Maggie said, "Yes! I don't like it anymore. It is more fun to stay on the beach. There is nothing to do in the mountains. My vote would be to sell it."

Nick sat there very quiet for a while. Then he asked, "If we sell it, does that mean we would never be able to go there again?"

"Yes, Nick. We would not go there again because it would belong to someone else," Vickie explained.

"Could we go to other mountains?" he asked.

"Sure. We could go on a vacation sometime and go into the Cascade Mountains. There are lots of places east of here that we could visit. There is Mt. Hood, Detroit Lake, the Columbia Gorge along the river, Crater Lake, and even over the mountains into the eastern part of Oregon. It is beautiful over there and totally different than the beach or the mountains. There are places on the other side of the mountains that are like a desert," Vickie explained.

"That would be fun, Mom. How long could we be gone from home? I need to keep up with my sand dollars," Nick announced.

Vickie laughed and looked at Maggie for her reaction. Her expression showed that she was not really enthusiastic about taking a long trip with her mother and brother.

Vickie said, "Maybe Maggie could bring a friend with her to keep her company. We could be gone at least two weeks."

Maggie perked up at the mention of bringing a friend and nodded to her mom.

"Let's get back to the subject of the cabin, though. We would need to finish the work of putting indoor plumbing in, putting a refrigerator in, and having the electricity updated. Maybe we would even have to put a furnace in. That would make it much easier to sell. What do you think?" Vickie asked her kids.

"I vote yes!" Maggie said.

"I vote yes!" Nick said, very proud that he had a say in what happened in the family.

"Okay. I will talk to Mr. Morgan and see if he can do the work or recommend someone who can," Vickie said. "Thanks, kids. Is there anything else that we need to talk about while we are all here?"

"Can I keep painting my sand dollars if we go on a trip to the other mountains?" Nick asked.

"Sure, but you will not be able to bring all of your supplies with you. Maybe we will be able to look for other things that you can paint. You know, there are different kinds of wood and rocks that you might be able to paint," Vickie answered.

"Okay. Just as long as I can keep painting my sand dollars. You know, Mom, the sand dollar reminds people of Jesus when he was born and when he died. My Sunday school teacher, Mrs. James, told me that when I first began painting them. I took her one that I painted. I think I have gotten a lot better since then," Nick said very proudly.

"You have gotten a lot better since you first started. I am very proud of you, Nick. And I am very proud of you for giving one of your sand dollars to Mrs. James. I'm sure she appreciated it," Vickie commented.

Maggie had wandered off to call Jeannie and see if she would like to go on a vacation with them this summer. Maggie was excited about the possibility of traveling with Jeannie. It would not be boring with her along.

"What about my sign, Mom?" Nick asked. "I really need it!"

"Okay. There is a shop in Newport that makes signs. We can go there and see what they would charge to make you a real professional sign. Maybe you should have two of them. That way more people would see your sand dollars," Vickie told him.

"Good idea, Mom," Nick announced.

Maggie was excited about going on a vacation now that she knew she could take Jeannie with her. Jeannie was excited about going also, but Vickie had to talk to Jeannie's mom and make all the arrangements, and they had to figure out when they were going.

In the meantime, Spencer Morgan and his son had finished Vickie's new sewing room, and it was beautiful. He had done a beautiful job of making the addition look like it had always been on the house. He even cleaned up the yard, put down new sod where needed, and prepared flower beds for Vickie to plant.

On the last day that Spencer and Todd were there, Vickie asked them about finishing the work needed on the cabin in the mountains.

"We would have to see the place and give you an estimate of the work needed to be completed, but it sounds like something we could do. When would you be available to go up there and show us the place?" Spencer asked.

"The kids and I can go pretty much anytime. I would like to get it completed and on the market as soon as possible," Vickie explained.

"How about making a day of it on Saturday?" Spencer asked. "I have a busy schedule for the rest of this week, and that would be the first day I would be available." He looked at Todd for his agreement to the plan, and Todd nodded yes.

"That would be great. Before Dan died, he bought a lot of the supplies he thought would be needed to add another electrical line for the refrigerator, so those are available for your use," Vickie told them.

"We will look at it and determine what we would need. Permits would be needed from the county before any work would be started. Is the cabin still in Lane County?" asked Spencer.

"Yes, it is about halfway between here and Eugene and 3 miles north on a narrow county road. You can follow us in your truck. We usually drove Dan's truck up there, so I know your truck will make it okay. The road does get a bit narrow closer to our property," Vickie explained.

Maggie asked her friend Jeannie to go to the cabin with them on Saturday. She didn't want to go without someone else with her. She was afraid all of the memories would make her cry, and with Jeannie there, it would help. Todd Morgan was going to be there, and Maggie did not want him to see her cry.

During the week before they went to the cabin, Maggie and the kids made a trip to George Parker's garden supply store to buy the shrubs and flowers needed for the new flower beds. Because there was a lot to plant, George said he would deliver them in his big truck, and maybe Vickie could put together a planting party. He and Shirley, his wife, thought it might be a good way to do a housewarming party for Vickie's new sewing room.

Since Vickie knew that she would need help in planting some of the larger shrubs, she said yes to the idea and made a date for the Saturday after their trip to the cabin. Now she would have to have the rest of the house ready for guests and make sure that the new sewing room was in order for people to see.

Both of the kids helped her move all of the boxes from the garage into the new room and open them to inventory the contents. Vickie had forgotten how much sewing stuff she already had.

Because of the great work Spencer had done in designing the room, she had cupboard and shelf space for almost everything she had. Vickie was probably most excited about the large built-in table that Spencer put in to cut fabric on and to put both her new sewing machine and new serger on.

She was anxious to start her new business and to be able to put all of her sewing supplies in one room and not have them in boxes in the garage. Her one regret was that Dan was not there to see all of this. He would have been so excited about her starting her own sewing business.

The trip that Vickie and her children, and Spencer Morgan and his son Todd, took up to the cabin on Saturday turned out to be more fun than any of them thought. Vickie, Maggie, and Nicholas were nervous about being there without Dan and upset about all the memories that they would have, but having Morgan and Todd there helped dissipate those feelings.

Morgan and Todd wanted to walk the property and see what was there. They knew that the cabin could be updated at minimal cost, especially since Vickie had the supplies needed to upgrade the electricity and the plumbing. Dan had purchased everything before he died, intending to do the work himself.

They all sat on a log outside of the cabin and ate the picnic lunch that Vickie had prepared for all of them and talked about the cabin and the land around it. Vickie owned almost two acres of forest land with the cabin right in the middle.

After lunch and another quick look inside the cabin, Morgan and Todd left to go back to Florence. Vickie had brought some boxes along to pack up the few personal items they had and take them home.

Vickie packed a box of Dan's tools that he always left there and a few heavy clothes that he had left. She had tears in her eyes as she did, but thought to herself that it was time to give it up. The three of them all had new memories to make. They would cherish the memories of their times there, but it was over.

With a packed car, the Roberts said goodbye to the cabin in the woods and headed back to Florence. When they arrived home, each of them took the boxes of their own personal items to their bedrooms, and Dan's tools and clothes were left in the garage.

Vickie took the kids out for pizza that evening. She had no desire to cook dinner, and they were all hungry for pizza.

When they got home, Vickie went to her bedroom to unpack the box of her personal items from the cabin and found an envelope with some pictures in it. They were pictures of her and Dan before the kids were born. Her memories came rushing back of days they spent pounding nails, getting shelves and cupboards up inside so that Vickie could put pots and pans away. And there were memories of nights spent in each other's arms, praying that the baby inside Vickie would be born healthy and happy.

Vickie looked at all of the pictures, tears running down her cheeks with each new picture, saying a final goodbye to the cabin and their life there. She fell asleep on her bed, fully dressed, with the pictures all around her.

Maggie and Nick came into her room to say goodnight, and Nick was ready to be tucked in. But when Maggie saw that her mom was asleep and saw what the pictures were, she quietly led Nick out of the room.

"Let's let Mom sleep, Nick. She has had a long day. I will tuck you in. You know I love to tuck you in," Maggie said with a sinister look in her eyes.

Nick started to run for his bedroom door, but Maggie caught up with him, tickling him as he tried to get into his room and close the door. She was right behind him, following him to the bed, tickling him mercilessly.

"Stop!" Nick laughed as he burrowed under his covers.

"You are my baby brother, and I want to give you a kiss!" Maggie laughed, moving down to kiss him on his cheek.

Finally, the roughhousing stopped, and Nick asked, "Is Mom okay, Maggie? She's not going to die and leave us like Dad did, is she?"

"She's okay, Nick, and no, she is not going to die and leave us. She is just really sad right now because today was her last trip to the cabin. We are going to sell it, and we won't be able to go there anymore. Mom has a lot of memories of the cabin and being there with Dad," Maggie explained to Nick.

"Okay, Maggie. Sometimes I get worried, though," he explained to his sister.

"Don't worry, Nick. I will always be here to take care of you, and someday you will be big enough to take care of yourself," Maggie said as she tucked the covers in around Nick and turned his light to dim. "Goodnight, Nick!"

The next morning, Vickie woke up startled that she had slept all night in her clothes. She didn't hear any noise coming from either of the kids' bedrooms or the kitchen and assumed that they were still asleep. She picked up all of the pictures scattered about, put them back in the envelope, and set them on her dresser. Then she stripped and went into the bathroom for a shower. She would have time to make the kids a good breakfast before they all went off to church.

When they returned from church, Maggie and Jeannie, and Nick and one of his friends from school wanted to go to the beach to look for sand dollars. It was late in the day to find any good ones, but they all wanted to go, so Maggie gave her permission, letting them know when supper would be ready.

While the kids were gone, Spencer Morgan called. She assumed he had a bid on the cabin updates and was glad that he was getting back to her so soon. The updates needed to be done before she could put it on the market.

"Vickie, Todd and I were talking about the cabin and the property you have, and we would like to buy it from you. We both think that it would be a great place for us to go to hunt. Both of us like to hunt for deer and elk in the fall, but neither of us likes to sleep in tents. The cabin would be a great place to live while we are hunting," Spencer informed her. "Todd is going to the University of Oregon in September, and the cabin would be an ideal place for him to use also. We were talking about some of the ways that we could add on and change the configuration of the bedrooms, so we would buy it the way it is now, without the updates being made first. What do you think?"

"I am in shock. I didn't anticipate putting it on the market until the fall when all of the improvements were made, but it would be just as easy to sell it now, I suppose," she pondered.

"Both Todd and I think that the price you are asking is a fair price for the cabin and the property. We are prepared to make a cash offer for the full price you are asking for the property," Spencer stated firmly.

"I am really in shock and can't believe that it will be as easy as this. I have the free and clear deed to the land, but I never did take Dan's name off of it. I do have the death certificate, so it shouldn't take too long to get the clear title. I will talk to my attorney and ask him about clearing the deed. My attorney is Gregory O'Toole. He has his office in Eugene," Vickie explained.

"I know Gregory. He is one of the group of men who hunt with Todd and me," Spencer said with amazement. "I have never used him as my attorney, but I know he is good. Give me a call when he clears the title; probably all we will have to do is go to the title company, sign some papers, and transfer money. Thanks very much, Vickie. Both Todd and I are excited about owning your place in the mountains."

# EPILOGUE

——— ✦ • ✦ • ◆ • ✦ • ✦ ———

*I*t has been two years since Dan Roberts died of a massive heart attack. Vickie Roberts has been able to keep the house and even add on to it with the inheritance her parents left her, the money from the sale of Dan's lumber business, and the money from the sale of the land and cabin in the mountains.

All of the damage caused by the tsunami that hit the Oregon coast, especially Florence and some of the small towns nearby, has been cleaned up. There have been a few tsunami warnings since that big one, but nothing has come ashore to cause as much damage as that one did.

Vickie Roberts started her own business making women's clothes. She is a very good seamstress and is able to put together different patterns to make unique garments that aren't found in ladies' dress shops. She has also made some beautiful wedding dresses, and more and more brides-to-be are contacting her about making their dresses. She has never had to advertise her business. Word of mouth has been the best advertisement for her.

Maggie is a senior at Florence High School and will attend the University of Oregon in Eugene in the fall. She is a very good student and has made top grades throughout her high school years. She wants to become a special-ed teacher.

Nicholas Roberts is 12 years old. Nick is in the sixth grade in the special education class at Florence Elementary School. He struggles with his work but is a very good artist.

Nick has painted his sand dollars for 2 years now and continues to sell them at George Barnes' IGA Grocery Store and a few other gift shops in the city. He believes that sand dollars are magic and he continues to tell anyone who will listen about the story of the sand dollar and how they symbolize the life of Jesus. The paintings that Nick does on his sand dollars are almost always of the sky and the sun shining on the ocean or of the moon shining down on the ocean and the sand. Nick says that if you look hard enough, you will see Jesus in each of the painted sand dollars.